# MAKING LIGHTNING

# MAKING LIGHTNING

## Restoring the Lost Art of Wonder

**MATT PETTRY**

*To Patrina:*

IF I'M KNOWN IN THE GATES,
IT'S BECAUSE OF YOU
(PROVERBS 31:23).

# CONTENTS

FORWARD   9

INTRODUCTION   11

### PART ONE:

## INTO THE STORM:
## RECEIVING WONDER

1. Into the Storm Cloud   19

2. The Way of Wonder   27

3. Avoiding the Invitation to Indifference   39

4. Hunger   51

5. Melted   59

6. Praying on Patmos   69

7. Praying Like A Son Of Thunder   83

8. Seek My Presence   95

9. New Clouds Of Unkowning   107

10. Strike the Ground   119

## Section Two:

# FROM CLOUD TO GROUND: RELEASING WONDER

11. Agitated By Storm    131

12. Red Skies At Morning    141

13. The Upper Room Gate    153

14. Priesting Before the Lord    161

15. Wind Always To Your Back    173

16. Lost in Wonder and Guided by Glory    185

17. Release the Sound    195

18. Sustaining Wonder    205

Notes    209

Bibliography    209

# FORWARD

I N OUR POSTMODERN RELIGIOUS CULTURE it is unusual for a book to be placed in our hands that was fashioned from the furnace of pure devotion. Therefore, this is far more than another script intended to entertain an amusement- saturated generation. To those who will dare to journey into the majesty of the Fathers throne, this is pure fuel for the heart burning for the real, the genuine and the authentic!

If you are sick of normal, weary with trying to pacify your holy cravings and tired of complacency posing as Christianity, brace yourself; you are about to experience the flaming heart of God calling you and I back to first love, back to holy fire. If you like your life the way it is turn around and go back, but if something in you is desperate for something so much more, then get ready, it's time to make lightning!!

Yahweh, raise up an army of Holy revolutionaries fueled by the fear of The Lord and filled with the thunderings of awakening!

*Damon Thompson*

# INTRODUCTION

———

THERE IS A MEDIEVAL PROVERB that says, "If a man's life be lightning his voice will be thunder." What does it mean to have a life like lightning? Lightning cannot be ignored. It's anything but boring. It evokes wonder. To me, having a life like lightning calls me to live fully alive to the glory of God. It's about living in wonder as a result of encountering the stunning beauty of Jesus and then allowing your awe-struck heart to become the greatest energizer in devotion. We need to recover the wonder of it all. We can receive this grace in devotion by cultivating interior wonder, lightning on the inside.

It is commonly held in the scientific community that the air around a single lightning bolt can reach 54,000 degrees Fahrenheit, making it the hottest natural substance on earth and fives times hotter than the surface of the sun. In order to produce the hottest-hearted disciples, we must get them around the hottest substance, the lightings of God. The place to encounter God's lightning is at His Throne where He is seated in wonder.

Wonder can be defined as that which causes astonishment, surprise, admiration, and amazement. It is astonishment or marveling at something awesomely mysterious or new to one's experience. So, wonder is a response. Specifically, wonder-filled-worship is our response when we have an encounter with beauty. For me, Supreme Beauty is found in the heart of the One who created everything beautiful in its time. Beauty is Jesus' idea. When we encounter Him our response is wonder-filled-worship. Wonder is our response to beauty.

> *"This is from the presence of Lord Yahweh and it is a wonder in our eyes!"* (Ps. 118:23)

We have access to the holiest place in existence through the holiest substance in existence, the precious blood of Jesus. Through His blood, we come boldly to God's throne and have our very own "Revelation 4" encounter with His majestic wonder. There is no place in existence with more wonder and intensity than the presence of Jesus. We need to allow His lightning to flash across our dull hearts and to allow His thunder to shake us from apathy.

It is this fixated wonder that we want to steward well. I don't believe the wonder in my heart for Jesus has to ever become dull. I want to live fascinated by Him. I want to walk in that fire of first-love devotion to Him, to grow in Christ-likeness, and to be found worthy to walk out God's highest purposes for my life. I believe this is possible for any saint who will allow God to strike their hearts with His majesty as He releases lightning and thunder from His throne.

*Making Lightning* is about positioning the heart to encounter the majestic beauty and glory of Yahweh. It is the process of being transformed by the glory of The Lord, responding with wonder-filled-worship, becoming fully alive, and releasing that wonder to others. *Yahweh makes lightning; we crumble in wonder.* But we must have another look. We are wrecked by His goodness but long for more of Him. His beauty strikes the heart with awe-filled wonder as we cultivate a fully awakened devotional life and then release Yahweh's majestic glory to others. Encountering God's presence through devotional-lightning will not only enable us to walk in the fire of first love, but will also empower us to release a sound (a thunder) that will awaken a sleeping generation.

The first section, *Into The Storm: Receiving Wonder,* we'll discover several key heart postures that position us to receive a wonder-filled heart from the glory of God. These attitudes of the heart energize devotional pursuit. We will also use John the Beloved as a character profile for what it means to be a person living fully alive to God. Using John as our profile, we give the call for *Devotional Reformers* to introduce to this generation a new paradigm of "New Testament" devotion to Jesus. At the end of each chapter we'll introduce spiritual disciplines and heart postures that position us to live with a sense of wonder called *Receive the Charge*.

In the second section, *From Cloud to Ground: Releasing Wonder*, we're calling the reader to take this sense of wonder public. Specifically, we show how wonder strengthens prayer and worship gatherings, provides direction for evangelism, and sparks a spirit of faith when believers come together. We'll see how the Upper Room of Acts 1 and 2 is a perfect picture of individual disciples bringing their measure of wonder together to release in prayer until God releases them in power. The Upper Room was the first solemn assembly with full access beyond the veil, and it is the launching place of the Kingdom through the early church. We cover details of what I believe the Book of Acts saints did that strengthened them as a praying community and how their sense of adventure bore them along as witnesses. Finally, I give a call to put believing prayer at the forefront of solemn assemblies.

You'll notice that some chapters have a different rhythm to them. One chapter was written at the historic Cane Ridge Meeting House near Paris, KY. One chapter was written on a ten-day retreat in the Daniel Boone Forest. One chapter was written in the Asbury Seminary library. One chapter was written in a prayer room. Other chapters were written from a small table in the children's ministry at our church

(I suppose to connect to childlike faith and wonder). The places where I have written share atmospheres; they were all empty with no one around. Perhaps creating a free and empty space for God to fill is what I was aiming for. I've tried to write the book I've always wanted to read. After grad school, Bible College, and pastoring I still find myself going after one thing: the glory of Jesus and His presence. I pray that *Making Lightning* serves His purposes and adds to His inheritance by producing the hottest-hearted disciples marked by His lightning.

Part One

—

# INTO THE STORM: RECEIVING WONDER

—

*And the smoke of the incense, with the prayers of the saints, ascended before God from the angel's hand. Then the angel took the censer, filled it with fire from the altar, and threw it to the earth. And there were noises, thunderings, lightnings, and an earthquake.*

(REVELATION 8:4-5)

—

# 01.

# INTO THE STORM

POSITIONING THE HEART
TO ENCOUNTER WONDER

—

LIGHTNING DOES STRIKE TWICE in the same place. In fact, there is a place that lightning strikes again and again night and day. It is the highest seat of power and the holiest place in existence. As such, the purest form of worship surrounds it. No worshipper there gives a half-hearted song. There are no "Jesus is My Homeboy" t-shirts worn where elders throw down their crowns. That lightning proceeding from the throne of Jesus keeps everyone guessing. Who can predict the path of lightning? Worship in heaven is unpredictable, immersed in the fear of the Lord, sparking awe-filled wonder in the saints, elders, and angels. No one just sings songs there. They tremble. They are so caught up in God's splendor that most of them just repeat themselves; *"Holy, Holy, Holy is the Lord."* Encountering the sights and sounds surrounding the throne enables any bored song-singer to recover the wonder of it all. There is a beautiful storm all around His throne. Enter the wonder-filled storm and receive devotional lightning.

Many do not consider this, but the Book of Revelation is a glimpse into an Apostle's devotional life. He was a human being, just like you and I named John. He begins the book saying *"I was in the Spirit on the Lord's Day,"* and ends the book with an *"Amen. Come quickly Lord Jesus."* So, reading Revelation is really a glimpse into a lightning-hearted disciple's prayer closet. John has released wonder-filled-worship at the holiest place in existence, God's throne, and as a result, returns from Heaven with thunder on his words to change the world.

## POSITIONED TO ENTER THIS
## WONDER-FILLED STORM

First, John the Beloved referred to himself as the disciple whom Jesus loved. I cannot overemphasis how important it is for you to be rooted in your identity as "Beloved" for the life of devotion. Secondly, John's statement, *"I was in the Spirit…"* doesn't mean that he was in the natural realm and then suddenly entered the realm of the Spirit, the realm of wonder. An actual rendering of this verse suggests that John *"came to be* in the Spirit."  John positioned himself to be in the Spirit.  John did not encounter the throne of Yahweh by sitting around waiting for something to happen.  He positioned himself in devotion.  We can position ourselves in devotion so that we may *"come to be in the Spirit."*  John was making lightning on the inside.  He was positioning himself in the Spirit.  More specifically, he knew that he was dearly loved by Jesus and then began cultivating devotional intensity before God through prayer and solitude on Patmos. The result of positioning himself in the Spirit enabled him to worship before the throne and return in the power of the Spirit.  I like to say he was becoming the Lord's vent.

## DEVOTIONAL REFORMERS

Lightning is formed because of an unbalanced electrical charge in the atmosphere during a storm.  A person full of interior lightning becomes that way because they've embraced an unbalanced devotional lifestyle in the wonder-storm.  It was a storm that made a sixteenth century reformer named Martin Luther.  He responded to the call of God on his life during a real lightning storm that almost took his life. He was so terrified by the strikes flashing closely by that he cried out to God to save him. He vowed that if the Lord would spare his life from the storm he would become a monk, and so he did. But the pressure wasn't off. After entering the rigors of monastic life, Luther would become a reformer as he gave himself to relentless search for God in Scripture and an overhaul of his own devotional life. His unbalanced devotion to Jesus over tradition, while sparked by a natural storm at first, would eventually produce a spiritual storm, an unbalanced hunger for truth. Luther lived out the proverb, *"If a man's life be lightning his voice will be thunder."*

Luther began to vent those fiery truths of the bible that had kindled in his heart with the boldness of David facing Goliath. He took the hammer of God's word and nailed his arguments to the Castle Church door in Wittenberg, Germany on All Saints Day 1517. This event sparked the Protestant Reformation. What Luther saw in the Scripture was vastly different than what the religion of his day forced upon him. The truth of God's word was like a volcano in Luther's heart and the result was a man venting through preaching, writing, praying, and reforming culture. I believe we are in desperate need of tenderhearted devotional reformers today that reform the Church to a Kingdom expression focused on the beautiful King.

When a person with a bright heart and conviction on

their words encounters the wonder realm of God, we've got a messenger, a builder, a discipler of nations. In Revelation 4, John stood in the stormy presence of God on His throne. John said, *"From the throne came flashes of lightning, rumblings and peals of thunder"* (Rev. 4:5). It is no surprise that John came out of this experience with a life as lightning and words as thunder to the church and the culture.

Can you imagine being the first person to talk with John when he got off the island of Patmos? Can you imagine his "Beyond-the-veil-confidence" to deliver those prophecies to the seven churches in Asia Minor? After his encounter at the throne, can you imagine John's resolve to see Jesus glorified in the nations of the earth? I don't think there is a church today ready for that John. Perhaps, it's that wonder-struck John we need the most. This man had just been to the stormy throne of God, saw unique manifestations of the beauty of Jesus, heard Him call the churches to be triumphant overcomers, heard Him declare what He values in those believers, heard Him warn believers that their names could be blotted out of the Lamb's Book of Life, and heard Him warn churches that their Lampstands could be removed. This man was a lightning bolt. John was anything but balanced. What would our response be today if John walked into our churches fresh from Patmos?

## GET BACK IN YOUR CAGE

Devotional reformers are always told, *"it doesn't take all that."* But they've entered the storm and encountered the wonder of Jesus. They are no longer bent toward backsliding. It is as if they've been magnetized toward Jesus on the throne. They're wonder struck. The demonstration of His love on the cross has stirred them to respond with whole-hearted obedience. When they are told *"It doesn't take all that,"* it sounds to these wonder-filled-worshipers like *"Get back in your religious cage."* That's not happening.

They believe that our secret place can look like the book of Revelation and that our walk with Jesus can look like the book of Acts and beyond. They've refused the taming of religion. An encounter with the wonder realm released lightning before their eyes and filled them with lightning on the inside. This interior lightning and internal flame must have a vent. The Lord's vent, that is what a witness for Jesus is. That is what a reformer is. A reformer allows the Lord to vent through them to impact change for God's glory in the lives of others.

> *"The lamp of the body is the eye. Therefore, when your eye is good, your whole body also is full of light."* (Luke 11:34)

Of course, reformers must start the reformation with themselves. They've allowed the candle of the Lord to thoroughly search their darkest places, received grace to change, and have become a change agent for the Kingdom. Surely, they've allowed Jesus to mantle them with His jealousy. It is real to them that they belong to a God who refuses to share them. Jesus has great desire to protect what is precious to Him and to remove anything that hinders loyal love. So this pure jealous lightning in their heart comes out, or vents with thunder; it is going to be heard.

## RECEIVE THE CHARGE

1. Can you identify storms in your life that impacted your devotion to God? Did you shrink back or did the storm actually push you more toward God?

2. What is it that you burn for? Can you identify your burdens; the things that you want to see set right? Ask the Lord how you can become the Lord's vent.

3. What is it that you do to position yourself in the Spirit?

"*The World is not lacking in Wonders, but in a sense of Wonder.*"

G.K. CHESTERON

"*I do not think there is anyone who takes quite such a fierce pleasure in things being themselves as I do. The startling wetness of water excites and intoxicates me: the fieriness of fire, the steeliness of steel, the unutterable muddiness of mud. It is just the same with people... When we call a man 'manly' or a woman 'womanly' we touch the deepest philosophy.*"

G.K. CHESTERON

# 02.

# THE WAY OF WONDER

ENERGIZING DEVOTIONAL PURSUIT

---

I PROBABLY WOULDN'T TAKE THE MOST valuable moments in history to tell people about ants, flowers, dirty dishes, sheep, goats, and soil fertilizer but this is exactly what we find the Lord of Life doing during His 3 short years reconciling the world to Himself. It's the most important time in history, God is walking the earth, every second counts, and He chooses to show his disciples where the fish are biting. He speaks about ordinary things in life and shows the disciples how they are windows into the Kingdom realm. I'm telling you, Jesus is a wonder. I believe that Jesus is fascinated with all of life. If He isn't, why did create it as He did?

We often forget that things like laughing, joy, and "a sense of beauty" all come from God. Think about that for a second – where did the sense of beauty come from if not from our Creator? How do you look at a painting, a mountain, or a river and say, "That's beautiful"? Who told you it was wonderful? The sense of beauty and wonder are perhaps the greatest proofs for the existence of God. But that's not my point right now. Right now I just want to marvel at the Person of Jesus, who walked around showing the "uncommonness" of common things.

There is a realm where we are carried away at how He made the water wet and mud muddy. We marvel over His idea to make laughing sound like it does. He didn't have to do any test runs to see if he liked it. Laughing came out of the joy He shares with the Father and the Spirit and all of our laughter echoes that reality. He even went overboard and gave some of us a contagious laugh (You know that friend that has a funny laugh that makes others laugh too). It makes me believe that Jesus is the one with the contagious laugh within the Holy Trinity. But that's just me. I believe Jesus stepped fully into the human condition, into this fallen world filled with darkness, and rubbed eternal bliss in our faces without apology. Consider the weight of these words spoken from Life Himself: *"…my joy will be in you"* (John 15:11).

I'm not asking you to find wonder. I don't think you find wonder. I believe you get lost in it. You turn aside to stop and stare. If you gaze on the beauty of Jesus on His throne and His Creation you'll slip into marvelous light. If you never take the time to marvel there'll be nothing marvelous about you. It doesn't matter what challenges you face today, you can get lost in the wonder of it all.

In a very real sense, Heaven begins now for those filled with devotional wonder (Obviously, more Heaven comes later, but the Kingdom is in me now). The opposite is also true. A measure of Hell begins now for those who refuse to honor the beauty of the Lord. Choose to marvel at His glory and goodness. Be like the Seraphim and discover that the whole earth is filled with His glory. Ask the Spirit of Glory to expand your capacity for wonder and astonishment by seeing the "uncommonness" of common things.

Moses prayed it this way, *"Lord, show me Your glory."* Paul prayed it this way, *"I pray... that you may be able to comprehend with all the saints what is the width and length and depth and height – to know the love of Christ which passes knowledge; that you may be filled with all the fullness of God."* Today, this sounds to me like, *"Lord, expand my capacity for astonishment."*

Everything in this world came from something God created. His mark is on everything we could possibly touch in this world or in the furthest parts of space. Elizabeth Barrett Browning once wrote, *"Earth's crammed with heaven, and every common bush afire with God, but only he who sees takes off his shoes; the rest sit round and pluck blackberries."* We need a massive overhaul in the renewal of our minds to see His glory behind snowcapped mountains, muddy creeks, and willow trees. His creation is crammed with Himself.

There are so many things to discover about Him in His word and His creation. I'm not talking about finding things in the character of God that are not in agreement with the Bible. I'm talking about those truths of God in the Bible that are merely head knowledge to us. Saints, if the Virgin Birth of Jesus doesn't make your heart say "wow," then it's still head knowledge to you. We need to linger with truth, to search out its depths until the truth we know awakens worship in our hearts. Now that's the way of wonder.

## WONDER FUELS THE LIFE OF FAITH

*"Faith is the inborn capacity to see God behind everything, the wonder that keeps you an eternal child. Wonder is the very essence of life. Beware always of losing the wonder, and the first thing that stops wonder is religious conviction. Whenever you give a trite testimony, the wonder is gone. The evidence of salvation and sanctification is that the sense of wonder is developing."*

—OSWALD CHAMBERS

The life of faith is fueled by your ability to see and hear God in all of life. Even horrible situations can be turned around for God's glory. Like children, we trust easily. This sense of wonder keeps us childlike. The moment we are born into the family of God our sense of wonder begins to develop. It is this childlike faith that we must beware of losing.

Nothing will dull your sense of wonder more than sin. Sin obscures your sense of God. The word *obscure* basically means, *undiscovered*. I'm saying that sin makes you "ok" with the undiscovered dimensions of God's heart. Sin cools your zeal to know and love God. It dulls your sense of wonder, because it blocks your path to discovering uncharted waters of God's glory. Sin makes you satisfied with the undiscovered dimensions of God's heart and Kingdom. It doesn't matter how the sin manifests, it begins with a cooling of our sense of God.

John Wesley's mother, Susanna Wesley, taught her children her definition of sin. She said, *"Take this rule: whatever... obscures your sense of God, or takes off your relish of spiritual things; in short, whatever increases the strength and authority of your body over your mind, that thing is sin to you, however innocent it may be in itself."* The life of faith is fueled by wonder, an eager anticipation and joyful adventure in Jesus. When you feel wonder wane, realign your convictions to the truth of God's word, turn from sin and trust Jesus again.

## CULTIVATING
## A WONDER-FILLED HEART

*"You called, you cried, you shattered my deafness.*
*You sparkled, you blazed, you drove*
  *away my blindness.*
*You shed your fragrance, and I drew in my breath,*
  *and I pant for you. I tasted and now*
*I hunger and thirst.*
*You touched me, and now I burn with*
  *longing for your peace."*     –SAINT AUGUSTINE

We will never pursue God consistently without it being real to us that He is pursuing us. Our love for Him is always a response to His love for us (1 John 4:19). Our cry for awakening and our efforts at evangelism are always responses to His great love for us and for others. Whatever reach we have for God is always a response to His reach for us. We simply have this desire to love Him back, no matter how small or weak it is, we want our love-back-response to God's love to be real. I'll grant that on my best days my love may be weak, but its real.

Augustine has said, *"You sparkled, you blazed, and drove away my blindness."* God takes the initiative to call, to shine, to shed His fragrance, to touch us, and we are motivated by His grace to respond. I wonder what kind of response we would give God back if He released grace to encounter His lightning. I think our hearts would be filled with wonder, fully alive, responding with childlike faith. Our reach for God may have some mundane moments, but every now and then, God releases a flash of light to spark our hearts with majesty again.

There is a story between two desert monks that show us what it looks like to be a disciple of Jesus marked by lightning. Abbot Joseph of Panephysis lived in the desert in the fifth century. He recorded this conversation between two of his fellow Desert Fathers:

> *"Abba Lot went to see Abba Joseph and said to him, 'Abba, as far as I can, I say my little office, I fast a little, I pray and meditate, I live in peace and as far as I can, I purify my thoughts. What else can I do?' Then the old man stood up and stretched his hands toward heaven. His fingers became like ten lamps of fire and he said to him, 'If you so choose, you can become all flame.'"*

## JESUS IS OUR ONLY FIRE STANDARD

I want to become all flame. In order to become all flame we must realize that Jesus is the only fire standard. We have no other devotional life to compare to but His. We want to be like Him and no other. God has predetermined that we all conform to the image of His Son Jesus (Romans 8:29). We cannot compare our fire of devotion to our pastor's fire. We cannot compare our church or movement with another. The Apostle Paul rebuked the Corinthians because they compared themselves with themselves, to which Paul said, "they are not wise" (2 Corinthians 10:12).

Jesus is the only fire standard and the only one to which we measure our hearts. He is the all-consuming fire and in order to become "all flame" we must get near Him encountering His wonder. Let's adopt Augustine's prayer:

*"My whole heart I lay upon the altar of thy praise, an whole burnt-offering of praise I offer to thee... Let the flame of thy love... set on fire my whole heart, let nought in me be left to myself, nought wherein I may look to myself, but may I wholly burn towards thee, wholly be on fire towards thee, wholly love thee, as though set on fire by thee."*

I believe there is a grace available for devotional reformers to *wholly burn toward* Jesus and redefine what devotion looks like. All that you and I have to do is say *yes* to the process of making lightning; positioning ours hearts before the majesty and glory of God. Like John the Beloved, we are those reformers who will push the devotional boundaries beyond what other generations have said was the edge of the map. We will brave the throne of majestic glory and re-enter our place in history to proclaim the unsearchable riches of Jesus.

## ADVENTUROUS PRAYER

Sufficiently awakened with God's wonder in our hearts, we enter the world as change agents. During his time of prayer on Patmos, John saw incense mixed with the prayers of the saints rising before God and then being hurled back to earth (Revelation 8). Prayers on earth were ascending to God from a golden censor and then re-entering history, shaking the rebellious order with noises, thunderings, lightnings, and earthquakes. Prayer ascends, and then God inverts the censor to release thunder, lightning, and voices from His presence.

Seeing this process is the ultimate faith-builder when it comes to prayer. Nothing strengthens my faith for prayer than to know that Yahweh sees me and hears me, that He receives my incense, that my adventures in prayer are filling a bowl before His throne that will eventually be turned upside down and re-enter history. This builds my faith to live under the inverted bowl of adventurous devotion.

The calling of Yahweh in this hour is for His disciples to be engaged in those disciplines that position them before His throne and encounter His wonder. We are to offer prayer to Him there in that place of exploring His heart, nature, power, and love. Then we are to allow the lightnings and thunders of His throne to move our hearts as we engage His greatness. We will see our prayers, our very lives, re-enter history in demonstrations of His power and authority. If the rebellious order of our day will not hear our preaching, they cannot ignore our devotion. It is time to govern and guide redemptive history through solemn assemblies comprised of disciples who have each encountered raw glory.

## RECEIVE THE CHARGE

### *Five Ways to Begin the Way of Wonder*

1. **Read aloud the biblical narratives of God's throne** (Revelation 4; Isaiah 6; Ezekiel 1). Reading the bible aloud helps to focus your mind and heart on the passage. Meditating on the Word means, "to chew" on the word, it needs to be in your mouth. It also makes it easier to begin to pray-read the passage (stopping at key points to pray the scriptures, ask the Lord questions, and declare praises to Jesus for who He is). Ask the Lord, "What did Ezekiel see? What did Isaiah see? What did John see?"

2. **Ask to Encounter the Fear of the Lord.** Here are some starters:

   *Father, put Your fear in my heart so that I will not depart from You* (Jer. 32:40).
   *Father, unite my heart to fear Your name* (Ps. 86:11).
   *Jesus, like you I want to delight in the fear of the LORD* (Isa. 11:3).
   *"Father, release the spirit of the fear of God into my heart. Release the lightning and thunder from Your throne to strike*

*my heart (Rev. 4:5) with Your majesty, that I might live in awe before You. Release Your presence and holy dread that makes me tremble before You. Unite my heart to your heart and Word and cause me to delight in the fear of God."* -MIKE BICKLE

### 3. Meditate on God's Majesty in His creation.

*The heavens declare the glory of God; And the firmament shows His handiwork. Day unto day utters speech, And night unto night reveals knowledge. There is no speech nor language where their voice is not heard. Their line has gone out through all the earth, And their words to the end of the world* (Psalms 19:1-4).

*For since the creation of the world His invisible attributes are clearly seen, being understood by the things that are made, even His eternal power and Godhead, so that they are without excuse...* (Romans 1:20).

### 4. "Come to be" in the Spirit by praying in the Spirit at all times (Eph. 6:18). Praying in the Spirit is also prayer in-step with the Spirit (prayer in-line with the Spirit). I would even say that prayer in the Spirit is a way to pray "into the Spirit" realm. Try to spend an hour a day praying in the Spirit.

### 5. Keep a place of solitude with God. John was on an island, a place of solitude for the word of God. Having a secret place with God alone positions us to receive the Father's open reward.

*Awake, you who sleep, arise
from the dead, and Christ
will give you light.*

EPHESIANS 4:14


*The opportunity of a lifetime
must be seized within
the lifetime of the opportunity.*

LEONARD RAVENHILL

# 03.

# AVOIDING THE INVITATION TO INDIFFERENCE

## Seizing the Opportunity of a Lifetime

———

R IP VAN WINKLE IS A SHORT STORY written by Washington Irving in 1819 that covers the years just before and after the American Revolutionary War. Old Rip is a lazy guy who is constantly in trouble with his wife. So Rip decides to journey off into the woods to get away from her. On his hike in the wilderness, Rip discovers a group of men playing games and drinking. He doesn't ask who the men are but instead sneaks over and starts drinking their liquor. He then falls asleep and awakens to find that his gun has rotted, his dog is gone, and his beard has grown over a foot long. He goes into town and finds out that his wife is now dead, all of his friends have died in a war, and that George Washington's picture has replaced King George's in the town inn. As a result of drinking that mysterious intoxicating liquor, Rip Van Winkle has slept for 20 years, right through the American Revolutionary War.

> *"The most striking thing about the story of Rip Van Winkle is not merely that Rip slept for twenty years, but that he slept through a revolution... one that would alter the course of human history... **We must remain awake through a great revolution.**"*
>
> MARTIN LUTHER KING, JR. MARCH 31, 1968

That intoxicating drink for Rip Van Winkle so numbed him that he slumbered through the most historic moments of his life. Sure, he avoided arguing with his wife, but he also missed history. He traded his part in the revolution for an intoxicating drink that put him to sleep.

Spiritual sleep robs us of living life to the fullest and making memories with God. There is a zombie-like culture of numb "Rip Van Winkle's" sleeping through great times of spiritual change but God is forming messengers who have avoided the invitation to indifference and have allowed Jesus to infuse them with such a spirit of awakening that they will shake the intoxicated sleepers from the slumber with their sobering voices. Rip Van Winkle slept through a revolution. Could that happen to you? Is that happening to you? Are you numbing yourself with worldliness when you know you were born to live fully alive to God? You don't have to miss anything. You can remain awake, living fully alive, and make history. People in wonder are people fully present to the moment. Wonder keeps them wide-eyed.

## MAN FULLY ALIVE

Saint Irenaeus is one of the many voices from history that gave us a vision of living life to the fullest. He said, "The glory of God is man fully alive." Living fully alive is another way to describe the life filled with wonder. If we are to live fully alive we must avoid the invitation to live indifferent and unresponsive. Avoiding the invitation to indifference is a key attitude of the heart to living in wonder.

Jesus, the God-man lived fully awake to the Father's purpose, entirely present to the moment, glorifying the Father by living in awakening. Jesus is the resurrection and the life, and through Him we can wake up from this long night's sleep that's been causing us to miss out on God's best and highest purposes for our lives. It's time to encounter the majestic glory of God by living fully alive.

Have you ever wondered what it would be like to be

fully awake to what's going on in the realm of the Spirit across the nations of the earth? Just imagine having the veil of this world pulled back and seeing fully what John saw in Revelation 4, that activity going on around the throne, or to see angelic wars swarming in heaven similar to Daniel 10, where the Prince of Persia and Michael the archangel were in a battle? We know there is much going on in the realm of the Spirit. We even believe that the Kingdom of Jesus is advancing, but we've got to get honest with ourselves and ask, "Why are we living like we are so painfully unaware of it?"

We know that our lives can only find security and significance in Jesus, and yet we still feel so numb to His conquering love. It is as if we are drinking intoxicating liquor numbing us to His call to come away and be with Him, and thereby sleep through our greatest opportunities in life. We become indifferent to His presence and even worse, indifferent to His love. But there's a revolution rising, and we refuse to sleep through it. In fact, we intend to live fully alive and lead the charge.

## DEVOTIONAL REVOLUTIONARIES

The gospel of the Kingdom is a gospel of devotional revolution. It is the gospel of Jesus mighty victory over death, hell, and the grave, whereby we are ransomed from death and conquered by His love. In Him, we are no longer under the dominion of sin and we now can live in devotion to Him. The government of Jesus is breaking into the earth and will ultimately be the world's government when He returns. Until His Kingdom comes completely, it is now breaking into individual lives, communities, and nations causing revolution. By revolution we mean "a change in power structure," and Jesus is inciting a revolutionary riot against darkness, shifting people and nations from the dominion of darkness to His Kingdom of Light. The Son of God is fulfilling His purpose, to destroy the works of darkness. Every salvation is an individual revolution. A change in power structure has taken place.

Revolutionaries are people who avoid indifference and want to make memories, not sleep through the glorious storyline Yahweh is writing today. I want history-making memories with Him. I want to live daily awakened to the plans, purposes, and presence of God. I don't want to be like those disciples who slept while Jesus prayed in the garden. They didn't recognize that history was changing forever right in front of them.

"Don't sleep while Jesus prays" had to be one of the toughest lessons the early disciples had to learn. He said, "Could you not watch with me one hour? Watch and pray so that you don't fall into temptation…" (Matthew 26:40-41). They were about to receive something that would change them forever, something that would shake them from boring prayer and awaken them to seize their moment in history. They were about to know Him as the crucified Savior and Risen King. Jesus said, "I am He who lives, and was dead, and behold, I am alive forevermore..." (Revelation 1:18). After His death and burial, they witnessed the resurrection of Jesus and I'm sure they would never sleep while He prayed again. The revelation that *Jesus is Alive* is the key to avoiding indifference. He glorified the Father as a man fully alive. He is alive and can show up in your prayer closet, your church, or even your neighborhood. Jesus is real and He is fully aware of everything.

After encountering Him as the One who is alive from the dead, the disciples who slept while He prayed in the garden became constant in prayer in the Upper Room. What changed? They became alive to who He is and the opportunity of changing the world around them. They were so awake to the moment that their impact would spread the gospel to the nations and influence every Christian after them. Every Christian can and must trace their roots back to their prayer gathering in the Upper Room filled with disciples who were living in awakening.

## THE "FULLY ALIVE" MAKE HISTORY

We must not slumber through our opportunities to make

memories with our spouses, our families, or our God. After all, isn't that what real friends do, make memories together? Think of all of the times in the bible that God has said, "Remember when I…" God often calls our attention to those history-making moments when He speaks with us. Unlike the dumb idols of wood, silver, and gold, God can predict the future, speak into the present, and He enjoys recalling our memories together (Isaiah 40:18-22).

There is depth in our friendship with God when He comes and rehearses our love-legacy, our stories, and our memories. What prayer is more friendly than to smile at God and say, "Lord, remember when we…" Of course, God doesn't forget anything. But those who have chosen to live wide-awake cherish real conversation with their Creator. It's a key to their spark of wonder. To recall history-making memories is what old couples do, its what war Veterans do, its what awakened believers do.

Do you have a secret history in God? You can. Living wide-awake isn't automatic. Living in God's best and fullest plan isn't like winning in Vegas. The promises of God must be grabbed, appropriated by faith, and pressed-into. If we are going to live in God's best plan and promises, we must avoid the invitation to apathy and violently pursue the Kingdom of God and His promises for us. Avoid Rip Van Winkle's intoxicating liquor that causes us to slumber through life's greatest opportunities.

Biblical sleep can have a bad vibe to it. We are warned that the bridegroom may return unexpectedly while folks sleep (Matthew 25:5) or you might even fall from a window during a long sermon (Acts 20:9). While physical sleep can be a reward for living right, spiritual sleep must be avoided. Paul in challenging believers to embrace the seriousness of their calling sounds like an alarm clock when he urgently says, "...now it is high time to awake out of sleep..." (Rom. 13:11). To the church at Ephesus, Paul again gives the wake up call; "Awake, you who sleep, arise from the dead, and Christ will give you light" (Eph. 4:14). In fact, Jesus told his followers to be faithful and watchful "lest, coming suddenly, he find you sleeping" (Mark 16:36).

## THE TRADE OFF

Like Rip Van Winkle, many accept the invitation to be spiritually indifferent to the world around them and apathetic to their potential greatness in God. They end up going on a journey they hadn't planned and end up drinking whatever will numb the situation for a season.

The invitation to indifference works by "trade-off." The thought goes like this:

- You want to see something set right.
- You ask God how it can be done.

- You count the cost.
- You choose instead to sleep on it or you choose a quicker fix than what God has prescribed ("Trade-off").
- You miss making a memory. You miss something historic. You miss God's best.

What will a man give in exchange for his legacy, his history, or worse, his soul? "Trade-off" is one of the enemy's traps. He always wants us to think that God has a plan B for us. The enemy wants us to trade God's Plan A for his Plan B. It's a trade that never pays off. That bowl of soup may look appetizing, and it may resolve your temporary hunger pains, but to exchange with the devil is to lose your inheritance. "Trade-off" works like the snooze button on the alarm clock. Instead of rising to the moment that we are supposed to, instead we trade time to be awake for a lesser option of sleeping in. When we accept the invitation to trade the best for the lesser, we become passive, inactive, dull, and vulnerable.

Who is more vulnerable than a snoozing soldier? This is why the lukewarm are so vulnerable to sin, they've chosen to be numb, and their eyes are dim to the enemies approach. A "trade-off" doesn't sound so bad to them. They are too sleepy to read the fine print of the enemy's Plan B. Before they know it, they tragically feel far from the presence of God. But Kingdom people have a "trade-off" of their own. They have a determination to exchange a passive lifestyle for one of pressing in to God's presence. They've resisted the temptation to hit the spiritual Snooze Button and have chosen to glorify God by living a life of prayer and obedience, seizing opportunities to make history. Jesus calls this being "watchful." The watchful have shaken themselves from the slumber through prayer and wholehearted obedience. In a word, they have resolve.

## RECEIVE THE CHARGE

### *Avoiding Indifference*

1. Ask this question, "Am I living fully alive or are there areas in me lying dormant?" Make a list of dreams yet to be fulfilled, spiritual gifts that you long to be used in (I Corinthians 12), and spiritual fruit that you long to cultivate (Galatians 5).

2. Make memories with God by acknowledging who Jesus is and who you are to Him. Say this aloud, "I am fully-alive to God and I am dead to sin."

3. Rehearse your greatest memories of Kingdom life with Jesus in prayer. Say to the Father, "Remember when we..."

"*The one who seeks should not cease until he finds, and in finding he shall MARVEL, and having marveled he shall reign, and having reigned he shall rest.*"

CLEMENT OF ALEXANDRIA

# 04.

# HUNGER

## GIVING DESIRE WINGS

———

WHEN YOU HEAR THINGS LIKE, *"Seek my Face continually..."* (Ps. 105:4), *"Men should always pray and never stop..."* (Lk 18:1), *"Pray in the Spirit always..."* (Eph. 6:18), and *"Pray without ceasing..."* (1 Thess. 5:17), do you hear a call to discipline or do you hear the voice of someone longing for unbroken communion with you? In these verses I hear the heart of someone saying, "I could talk to you all day long. I don't want the communion to stop. You'll hang up first." You might want to reread these verses with the understanding that *"The Spirit that lives in us wants us to be his own"* (James 4:5 God's Word Translation). I know that we talk much about our longing and hunger for the Lord but have you considered the Spirit's longing for us? Our communion with the Spirit is the result of mutual longing.

William Seymour was desperate for the fullness of the Holy Spirit. He had such a hunger for more that he gave himself earnestly to the secret place five hours a day for two years. He wasn't satisfied. Seymour asked God, "What else can I do?" The Spirit spoke to him and said, "Pray More." Seymour then changed his five hours a day to now seven hours a day. He continued in secret prayer seven hours a day for another year and a half. The result was a glorification of the Spirit, not just in Seymour, but one that would have a historic impact called the Azusa Street Revival.

John G. Lake said of Seymour's hunger, *"God had put such a hunger into that man's heart that when the fire of God came it glorified him. I do not believe any other man in modern times had a more wonderful deluge of God in his life than God gave to that dear fellow, and the glory and power of a real Pentecost swept the world. He [Seymour] preached to my congregation of ten thousand people when the glory and power of God was upon his spirit, and men shook and trembled and cried to God. God was in him."*

When you hear this story do you say, "Wow, what a price?" or do you say, "Wow, what a communion?" Are we hung up on the price or in awe of the glory that came with that depth of communion in the Spirit? Make sure to listen to the Spirit's longing in this story, "Seymour, I want you to pray more."

The Spirit is longing for an unbroken communion with this man! What an honor?

Do you hear your name being called inside Seymour's witness? I believe Seymour positioned himself in the secret place for what we all should crave, the "Pray more," "the pray always," the place of unbroken communion with the Holy Spirit. The result was a glorification of the Holy Spirit for something historic and I'm so glad he responded to the Spirit's longing for him to "Pray more." The Holy Spirit's longing for communion wasn't going away. Seymour's longing for the Spirit wasn't going away. Don't ignore the longing. The feeling is mutual.

Give your desires for Jesus devotional wings. Give your desires eyes to see Him. Give your desires ears to hear him. I want you to give your desires wings. Give your desires arms and legs. Give them claws if you must. But do not waste another moment longing but not reaching.

> "Hunger is one of the most important signs of life. When there is no hunger for a sustained period, then there is no life. Many live in a "spiritual intensive care unit" without any hunger for prayer or the Word. This is abnormal Christianity. Hungerless and passionless Christianity is not normal from God's point of view. Lack of hunger is a serious sign of sickness in the spirit."
>
> -MIKE BICKLE

To hunger and thirst for righteousness is to hunger for our union to God, for proximity of the highest nearness, it is longing for His Presence. John G. Lake calls this righteousness we hunger and thirst for the "right-ness of God." It is the right-ness of life. Right-ness in devotion. Right-ness in your marriage. Right-ness in your body. The Right-ness of God in your business. John Wesley says that the righteousness we are to hunger and thirst for in Matthew 5 is nothing short of becoming the very image bearers of Christ on earth. The Orthodox tradition would say it is our deification, becoming Godly.

## VIOLENCE OF DEVOTION

In Matthew 11:12, Jesus reveals that those with hunger and determination for His Kingdom are the "violent" that aggressively lay hold of it. Jesus said, "The kingdom of heaven suffers violence," what did he mean? To "suffer" means, "to permit." When Jesus says, "Suffer the little children to come unto me," he is saying, "permit" them to come to me. In Matthew 11:12, Jesus is saying that the kingdom of heaven is permitting a violent approach to laying hold of it. And this is where we tend to lose some folks. They don't like this word "violent." But think of it as "Go for it!" And then take it one step further; "Go for Jesus and His Kingdom until He and His promises are in your hands." That's the "violence" we're talking about. It's violent to selfishness, pride, and worldliness but glorious to your heart.

The "violent" that Jesus speaks of in Matthew 11:12 are "devotionally violent." The violence of their devotion to Jesus has overcome the violence of opposition against them. The "yes" in their hearts to Jesus is greater than the "no" of opposition. In a word, they have hunger. They have passion. The fire of obedience to Jesus has unlocked the promises of the Kingdom to them. They are possessors of kingdom promises. I am so thankful that Luke wrote a parallel passage to Matthew 11:12 because it makes the meaning so much clearer.

> *The law and the prophets were until John. Since that time the kingdom of God has been preached, and everyone is pressing into it* (LUKE 16:16).

It is as if Luke is saying that every man storms his way into the kingdom, that no one just drifts into it, and that the kingdom opens up to those who are in eager pursuit of it. We need to awaken ourselves from reluctant apathy and embrace devotional hunger to see the Kingdom of Jesus reigning in our lives, cities, and nations.

Pressing into the kingdom of God is about making a choice to be hungry for what God loves, and what you love as a citizen of His kingdom. It is living wide-awake, refusing the invitation to be indifferent to God and his promises. It is living with our senses alive to God and dead to sin. It's a tenacity to protect the tenderness of your heart toward God and others. As we'll see in the next chapter, tenderness of heart towards God and others is a major result of a person who has been in the glory of God. The lightnings of God melt our hearts and make us tender. Lets see what that looks like.

## RECEIVE THE CHARGE

### *Ways to Live with Resolve*

1. **Be violent in devotion:** Spiritual disciplines are violent to the sinful nature. Giving is violent to the wallet. Prayer is violent to pride. Devotion is violent to our selfishness. Forgiving others is violent to our vengeance. Allow your devotion to Jesus to be greater than the opposition.

2. **Consistently Apply Principles:** Develop a rhythm to your time and stay with it. Have specific times for you to be alone with God.

3. **Add Expectation to Discipline:** Do you really believe that God hears you when you pray? Have anticipation that when you sow to the Spirit you will reap life. Many practice a devotional life but do not place a demand to receive grace for change. Believe that you receive when you pray.

—

*"The higher people are in
the favor of God,
the more tender they are."*

MARTIN LUTHER

—

05.

# **MELTED**

EXPERIENCING THE WONDER
OF FIRST LOVE

———

MOM USED TO MAKE CINNAMON toast for breakfast. It was her gift of awakening (it at least awakened my brother and I). Single working moms always develop a few tricks of the trade to get kids up for school, get ready for work, and making breakfast. The smell of that cinnamon, butter, and toasted bread was our alarm clock. It would hit your nose while you were snug under those covers and lure you to the kitchen no matter how deep in sleep you were. That toast was so good it could set the tone for the whole morning.

On rare occasion, when the morning would not cooperate, our beloved cinnamon toast would burn. The effect was the opposite of making us smile. We were mad. It's too crispy and smells smoky. Now, everything seemed to be off, and our attitudes began to show it. Have you ever been spanked in the morning? It's no way to wake up that's for sure. Burning toast can happen so fast. It has happened to everyone.

It's silly how life can get out of hand with little things like burnt toast. When our hearts and attitudes become dry, crispy, and smelling like smoke, nobody wants to be around us, because even little things throw us off. But when we are close to God we are quick to obey, quick to believe, and quick to repent.

When you are close to God your heart becomes tender and "easily-moved" by the voice of God. When we encounter the majesty of Jesus our cold and stony heart is melted. Like wax, we are warmed by the fire of God's love and become so pliable that we easily take the shape that God has for us. The heart melted by fiery love is a tender heart. You know you're in that place of tenderness when you feel the thrill of hearing the name of Jesus. When you're walking in tenderness toward God you can see a total stranger and suddenly be overwhelmed with compassion for them. Like Jesus, compassion will move you into an unshakable faith for others to receive a miracle (Mark 1:41).

Several years ago, I hit a season where I was rapidly becoming a piece of burnt toast. I was teaching five and six bible college classes a day, Monday through Friday. I was preaching on the weekends and on Wednesday nights. Also, I started teaching night classes at another college from 6PM-10PM one night a week. The grace was oozing out of me quickly, and my heart was getting hard. It happened so fast, just like burning toast. In essence, I was losing my sense of wonder.

I put the brakes on that busy pace, and decided to take some time and begin my search for that tender place again. My wife encouraged me, "You need to get away, go somewhere and hear from God." Thank God for wives that support the grace of God on their husband's lives. So, I got in my car and made the trip to a place I like to go when I need to shut down business as usual and hear from God.

I had one prayer, "God, give me a tender heart." Repeatedly, I prayed that prayer under my breath across the mid-west until I arrived at my destination. I wanted the movements of my heart to be entirely bent towards Jesus again. That's what it means to be a tender man before God. A tender man is a man moving towards God, following God, carried by God. I went into a room that this ministry had set up for corporate prayer, and I just tried to hide in the back. I didn't want to be bothered; I just wanted that tender place with God again. All day under my breath in that prayer room

I prayed, "God, give me a tender heart easily moved. Give me a heart moving towards you, bent towards you again."

The next day I attended a seminar, which had some personal ministry time after the session. One of the leaders attending the seminar looked at me and began to prophesy, "The Lord wants you to know that he's given you that tender heart you've been asking for." My eyes shut, my head leaned forward, and I sank in that chair as the Lord's confirming words melted my heart. It was as if the Lord granted me the tender heart the moment this messenger of the Lord released that word. I was a mess of tears, trembling, and tenderness. The leader continued to speak as I tried to gather myself in order to listen, "I see you with all these stars in your hands. You are holding them close to your heart like you're carrying them. The Lord is giving you a mantle to shepherd those stars. You are going to shepherd messengers." I sat there and cried.

After several minutes passed by, I finally gathered myself and decided to drive back over to the prayer room to try and process this word. I walked into the prayer room and the worship leader began singing a song I've never heard. The words on the screen read, "He who has the seven stars in His hand… He holds my heart. He holds my heart." My jaw dropped. In a completely different location, with different people, that word was chasing me. I'd been set up. In that moment God was giving me an immense honor to shepherd messengers, and I believe He wanted me to know the key to unlocking this mandate was to receive and maintain a tender heart that is continually bent and moving towards God. Maintaining a tender heart would be vital to my life and my assignment. Maintaining a tender heart would be the key to fathering stars.

## TENDERNESS UNLOCKS MOVEMENT

The melted, moving, tender heart is probably near the top of the list for being a messenger of God's Kingdom at the end of the age. Apostle, prophet, pastor, teacher, and evangelist become pieces of burnt toast without this tender place before God. The mere drama of people conflicts alone will take out many generals, building up in them a calloused heart if they don't maintain tenderness with God and people.

When you hear the word tenderness don't think of wimpy. Instead think of movement, think of passion. *Why?* Tenderness of heart is the opposite of hardness of heart. Hardness of heart always halts movement towards the promise (Hebrews 3:8). In fact, one synonym of hardheartedness is stubbornness, being unwilling to move. The way we get things moving is to get the stony heart of rebellion and stubbornness out of us and embrace the easily moved heart. Having a tender heart means that God's love has conquered our stubbornness, rebellion, and disobedience in such a way that we willingly and joyfully say, yes to God's every whim and whisper. He has all of us. Tenderness of heart always accelerates movement towards God and His promise. We cannot move forward unless we are pliable, flexible, even melted in the hands of God. In tenderness we discover His ways.

## THE FIRST STEP TOWARDS
## WHOLEHEARTEDNESS

Tenderness isn't the doormat. It's the doorknob. Do you want to see open doors into God's heart, into His plans and purposes? Those realities are opened fully through wholehearted obedience. Tenderness is the first step to wholehearted obedience. A tender man is actually a giant in the Spirit trampling his own pride and triumphing over those areas un-yielded to God. I would say that the tenderhearted are the cruelest people to darkness. *Why?* Rebellion and stubbornness cannot be found in them. Jesus revealed how His obedience to the Father was the reason why the enemy had no place in Him (John 14:30, 31). There was nothing in Jesus that was hardhearted or rebellious to the Father's plan. Jesus lived with a continual "Yes" in His heart to the Father, which moved Him into the Father's purposes and plans.

## WALKING IN THE WONDER
## OF FIRST-LOVE

*Therefore, as the Holy Spirit says: Today, if you will hear His voice, do not harden your hearts as in the rebellion, in the day of trial in the wilderness* (Hebrews 3:7-8).

*Who is she coming up from the wilderness leaning on her beloved? I awakened you under the apple tree* (Song of Solomon 8:5).

The Bride in Song of Solomon 8:5 is walking in the fire of first-love. Unlike those hardhearted rebels in the wilderness, she comes up victorious over the wilderness testing and is now dependently leaning on Jesus. She is not in front of Him or behind Him. She is led easily. She is joined to Him, depending on Him for every step. She has no rebellion, no hardness of heart; she is leaning on Jesus, walking in step with the Spirit, walking in obedience. When we learn to lean on Jesus we can come up from the wilderness victorious. Leaning on Jesus means that we understand our dependency upon Him and that we need Him. We express our dependency upon Jesus by engaging in those practices that position us to receive His grace, His enabling power, and His support.

We leave stubbornness and rebellion in the wilderness.

From that moment forward Jesus has a unique place He wants to take the conversation. After the bride in Song of Solomon 8:5 has victory over rebellion, the couple begin to rehearse their love-legacy. They reminisce; "Look over there at that apple tree... that is where I awakened you... that is where we first met." They remember the days of first love. Leaning on Jesus is her way of expressing wholehearted dependency. The tender place of dependency has positioned her to receive the love of Jesus and made her easily moved to obedience. The love of Jesus has worked its awakening power in her life. From that moment, their conversation is now focused on making memories together from the fire of first-love.

To me, tenderness of heart towards Jesus is the key to remaining in that place of devotion like we had at the beginning, at our first altar, when He first awakened us under the apple tree. Tenderness of heart is expressed through quick obedience to Jesus. *Tenderness, the opposite of stubbornness, is a picture of the heart easily moved towards Jesus, no longer bent towards backsliding.* The tenderhearted disciple is a lightning hearted disciple. A person close to the glory of God will always display a melted heart of love towards Jesus and others.

I believe John the Beloved exemplifies the lightning hearted disciple. Jesus turned this "son of thunder" into a man who can't stop talking about love, life, and light. John was the only disciple who forced his heart to fully take in what happened the cross. All of the others left Jesus at this point, but not John. He gazed more fully than any other upon Jesus' supreme act of love. I believe that this moment so melted John's thunderous heart that even in his most desperate times on Patmos he could engage love and lightning at the throne of Yahweh. It doesn't matter what you are facing, we can learn from John how to pray on Patmos.

## RECEIVE THE CHARGE

### *Three Ways to Cultivate the Tender-Melted Heart*

1. **Fasting:** Biblical fasting empties us so that we can be filled with God. It is our means to clean the house and make room for more of God. It enforces death to our flesh and stubbornness. When fasting, it becomes easier to say "no" to sin. This is because our body is becoming our servant and our inner man is ruling. When the inner man is in charge, our hearts always ready to obey Jesus

2. **Searching:** Ask the Holy Spirit to search you and see if there be any stubbornness in your heart. Look for the impasses, those places where you've seemed to hit a wall or a ceiling and ask the Lord if there is anything in your heart that's blocking movement.

3. **Calling:** Begin to make this your prayer, "God, give me a tender heart." I have experiential evidence that He will answer this prayer.

*I, John, both your brother and companion in the tribulation and kingdom and patience of Jesus Christ, was on the island that is called Patmos for the word of God and for the testimony of Jesus Christ. I was in the Spirit on the Lord's Day, and I heard behind me a loud voice, as of a trumpet, saying, "I am the Alpha and the Omega, the First and the Last," and, "What you see, write in a book and send it to the seven churches which are in Asia: to Ephesus, to Smyrna, to Pergamos, to Thyatira, to Sardis, to Philadelphia, and to Laodicea.*

(REVELATION 1:9)

# 06.

# PRAYING ON PATMOS

FIVE TYPES OF PRAYER
THAT POSITION US TO ENCOUNTER
GOD'S MAJESTIC WONDER

———

I LOVE WALKING ON A NARROW COUNTRY road at night with nothing but the moon and stars to help me see. The darker it is the brighter these lights shine. Walking in the middle of the night causes my other senses to be fully awake, trying to make up for what I can't see. Every crack in the nearby woods is heard. I can feel the contours of the dirt road right through my shoes as I shuffle my feet forward. I feel fully alive and dependent upon the small amount of light above me. I think this is what it feels like to pursue devotional wonder in our day. It's midnight, dark, and I'm depending on my awakened senses to keep me in the middle of the road with only moonlight to guide.

The devotional reformer today is like a man walking through our times on a narrow country road at midnight dependently moving forward with what light he has. Others grope about in the darkness, but he's caught up in splendor of the stars above. The wonder of morning keeps him excited. Put him in the wilderness, and he turns it into wonder. Surround him with darkness, and he'll see the testimony of God's creation in the moon and shooting stars. Turn him over to the elements of a barren wilderness island, and he'll turn on the seer dimension and gaze upon rainbows encircling a throne with One sitting on it whose appearance is like a jasper and sardius stone. The devotional reformer of today is a person of dependence. They are God-needy. The hostility of the world continually offers them the broad way, but they've found a hidden joy on a narrow country road of dependence.

It's quite possible that John the Beloved experienced this sense of devotional dependency while in exile. Patmos means "my killing." It is a name that this rugged and barren island wilderness deserves. It is not comfortable, but

Patmos is a great place to pray. John the Beloved turned his wilderness island into a place of wonder. He turned a place of "my killing" into a place of encounter with Jesus. Like walking on a dark country road at midnight, his spiritual senses came alive to the realm of awe-struck wonder.

Maybe you're in a place that seems to be "your killing." It may be a place of persecution, barrenness in prayer, or famines of God's presence. Or perhaps The Lord is calling you to put on the cross those areas of your life that are not like Him. Allow God to turn this around for His glory. Allow the place of "my killing" to become the place of "my deepest consecration." John turned Patmos into a prophetic encounter by "coming to be in the Spirit." We too can enter the realm of the Spirit right where we are and begin to see things from God's perspective. How do we do this? We pray in the Spirit. We pray ourselves *into* the Spirit.

Prayer is a means to show our dependency upon God and turn the dark places of our lives into devotional wonder. We can go into difficult situations a lowly Private and come out a decorated General, ready to change the world for Jesus if we'll express to God our great need of Him. I have found at least five ways to pray that will express devotional dependence to God and enable us to turn a Patmos into prophecy.

## TURNING PATMOS INTO PROPHECY:
### *Five Ways to Pray that Position us to Cultivate Wonder*

NUMBER ONE
## Cultivating Wonder through Meditating on Scriptures

The resurrection of Jesus makes Christian meditation different than any other religions form of meditation. Because Jesus is alive, the goal of our meditation is not to meditate on *nothing* but on *someone*. We do not seek to clear the mind but to fill it with wonder. Christian meditation is filling our minds with the Holy Spirit through the praying imagination (could be said of contemplation as well, I suppose). We sanctify our imagination as we put it in contact with the world of the bible, the Kingdom of Jesus, and God's creation.

To "meditate" means to reflect; to moan, to mutter; to ponder; to make a quiet sound such as sighing; to meditate or contemplate something as one repeats the words. The goal of Christian meditation of Scripture is to cultivate the mind of Christ and to make holy our thoughts (I Cor. 2:16; Phil. 4:8). We want to "Let this mind" be in us "as it was also in Christ Jesus" (Phil. 2:5). It is a way that we stay connected to the Word.

Our spiritual growth is directly connected to how much

bible we intake. Pray the bible, read it, listen to the bible on audio, write out verses, and immerse yourself in the Word. We are sanctified (or made holy) by truth; God's word is truth (Jn. 17:17). Since the Holy Spirit is the author of the bible (2 Tim 3:16; 2 Peter 1:20-21), He will never speak contrary to its principles, priorities, and purposes. The Scriptures provide us with language for our conversation with God. We develop a Word-shaped life as we engage the Scriptures with our imagination. Slip from your chair and enter the pages of your bible with all of your senses.

Here is a practical approach to meditating on scripture:

1. **Choose the Verse:** Pick a verse that the Lord is highlighting in your life.
2. **Write the Verse:** Slowly write out the verse. While writing out the verse, audibly say the words that you write.
3. **Read the Verse:** After you have written out the verse, slowly repeat the words.
4. **Memorize the Verse:** After you have read the verse and have some familiarity with the words, begin to recite the verse without looking at the Bible (you may just want to begin remembering the first few words or even the first word – repeat it audibly until you got it committed to memory).
5. **Pray/Meditate the Verse:** Once you have the

verse in your memory, begin to pray the verse. Pay attention to a word or two that is standing out to you and begin to pray the verse from your heart.

NUMBER TWO

## Cultivate Wonder through Practicing God's Presence

We begin our journey in practicing an awareness of God's presence by placing our confidence in the scriptures that promise us that God is everywhere. We simply pay attention to God and cultivate a loving gaze upon him throughout the day everywhere where we are. Said negatively, practicing the presence of God means that we never let our thoughts get far from Him.

We need to be clear that this is NOT merely imaginary. Practicing God's presence is acknowledging the truth that God really is everywhere. There is nowhere that He is not. Of course we are not speaking of His manifested presence but His essential presence. I do believe that renewing our minds to acknowledge the truth that He is everywhere essentially is the first step to seeing His manifested glory anywhere. We first become aware of His presence around us and in us. You can begin the journey of practicing God's presence by simply thanking God for His presence.

NUMBER THREE
## Cultivate Wonder through Praying in the Spirit

Praying in the Spirit is a means to pray into the realm of the Spirit, the realm of wonder. Specifically, I'm talking about praying in tongues for your devotional life. Every New Testament writer either spoke in tongues or was influenced by someone who did. I say this because every New Testament book is connected to an apostle. Every New Testament apostle that wrote a New Testament book was in that Upper Room where they testified that they "all" spoke in tongues (Acts 2:4) or they testified in their own writings that they did like Paul (I. Cor. 14:18). The only book I'm not certain about is Hebrews, and I'm not willing to say that it wasn't connected or influenced by a New Testament apostle. I like to tell people that if tongues was good enough for Jesus' Momma, then it's good enough for you. Yes, Mary the Mother of Jesus was also in that Upper Room (Acts 1:13-14) where it was said that they all spoke in tongues (Acts 2:4). The Mother of Jesus was a tongue-talker.

It is absolutely glorious when you use this devotional language for extended moments in prayer or throughout the day. The longer you pray in the Spirit the stronger your inner man will be. Praying in tongues in your devotional life will open up to you many dynamics of intimacy with God and personal edification. Some of the most commonly held benefits of praying in the Spirit are, personal edification (I Cor. 14:4), praying the will of God (Rom. 8:27,28), building up faith (Jude 20), and giving thanks well (I Cor 14:15-17). When we pray in the Spirit we are praying in-step with the Spirit. In our private devotions, we speak out mysteries, build ourselves up, we pray for what we do not know, and we praise and magnify God. Try to pray in the Spirit as much as you can. You can do this while you are doing other things, whenever you want, and as much as you want (its the safest way to pray while driving).

NUMBER FOUR
## Cultivate Wonder through the Prayer of Silence/Word-Fast

Silence enables us to hear. No one can listen well while they are talking. Silence will make you become more conscience of idle and negative speech. You may need to spend some time in absolute silence, but the goal is to hear not to just get quiet. Get quiet so that you can listen. A sustained position of wonder requires restrained conversation with man. Remain in wonder by setting apart your mouth for a holy purpose.

One of the greatest "fasts" I've ever been on happened

when I choose to not say anything unless I was spoken to for seven days. My goal was silence so that I can hear the voice of God more clearly. I was becoming aware of some of the negative things coming out of my mouth and I knew something needed to be adjusted in my heart, because it is out of the abundance of the heart that the mouth speaks. So I entered into silence. I wasn't rude to my family, friends, or co-workers. When they spoke to me I responded in brevity. I stilled the inward chatter of my heart and engaged a deep silence. I found that in the deep places of silence are wellsprings of wonder. It's downright hilarious how much joy is found in the cleansing bath of a wordless baptism.

If my silence doesn't bless you, then nothing I say can. People don't usually understand that, but they also can't deny that we're happy in God when this discipline is in place. Of course, we are not talking about being quiet so that we can ignore people or problems. This silence is not to keep us from confessing sin or shutting people out of our lives by giving them the silent treatment. We are simply engaging in silence so that we can abide in wonder. Consider these passages on silence:

*Hannah was praying silently; only her lips moved, but her voice was not heard* (I Samuel 1:13).

*After the earthquake (there was) a fire, but the Lord was not in the fire; and after the fire a sound of sheer silence* (I Kings 19:12).

*If you would only keep silent, that would be your wisdom* (Job 13:5).

*When you are disturbed, do not sin; ponder it on your beds, and be silent* (Psalms 4:4).

*For God alone my soul waits in silence; from him comes my salvation* (Psalms 62:1, 5).

*But I have calmed and quieted my soul, like a weaned child with its mother* (Psalms 131:2).

*The Lord is in his holy temple; let all the earth keep silence before him* (Habakkuk 2:20).

*Let everyone be quick to listen, slow to speak, slow to anger* (James 1:19).

NUMBER FIVE
## Cultivate Wonder through Breath Prayers

Never under estimate the power of three-second prayers. Just because you didn't feel anything when you said it doesn't mean it didn't move heaven. Throughout the day, release short prayers that flow as natural as breathing. You probably already have a short prayer that you pray regularly. You need to know that those short prayers throughout the day count just like long prayers in private. Begin to give thanks for everything. Quote or declare a promise from Scripture to God. Pray out a favorite verse of scripture. Many miracles in the bible were the result of a short faith-filled declaration. Pray short prayers asking God for revelation. Ask Him how to do things. He will teach us. Look at these short power-packed prayers:

*On the day the LORD gave the Amorites over to Israel, Joshua said to the LORD in the presence of Israel: "Sun, stand still over Gibeon, and you, moon, over the Valley of Aijalon (Joshua 10:12).*

*Speak Lord… for your servant hears (1 Samuel 3:9-10).*

*Father… into your hands I commit my spirit (Psalm 31:5; Luke 23:46).*

## RECEIVE THE CHARGE

There are many ways to cultivate wonder through our prayers. These five have been a treasure for many over hundreds of years of pursuing Jesus. I have found them to be especially helpful in turning the barren wilderness seasons into Patmos wonder.

John the Beloved turned Patmos into a prophetic encounter by engaging the Holy Spirit. He came to be in the Spirit and turned a desperate situation into something that redefined what was possible in a prayer life. His encounter with Jesus on Patmos stands as a witness to what a human being's devotional life can be. He is a devotional reformer. How did he get to this place of devotion? He spent years watching the Master at devotion. He listened to Jesus pray. He heard God talk to God. When you listen to Jesus pray it becomes real that God is a wonderful and involved Father. This truth is the simple way that Jesus made devoted disciples. If you wonder why the fire is low and why devotion is weak, we begin here, seeing God as a wonderful Father. Let's listen to Jesus pray.

Here's again are the five ways to turn those difficult places into places of revelation and encounter:
1. Meditating on God's Word and His World.
2. Practicing God's Presence.
3. Praying in the Spirit.
4. Engaging the Heart in Silence.
5. Praying Short Breath Prayers Throughout the Day.

———

*and has made us kings and
priests to His God and
Father, to Him be glory
and dominion forever and
ever. Amen*

(REVELATION 1:6)

———

07.

# PRAY LIKE A
# SON OF THUNDER

ENCOUNTERING YAHWEH
AS A WONDERFUL FATHER

———

I LOVE TO HEAR LEADERS PRAY MORE than hearing them preach. You can learn a great deal about a person by listening to them pray, how they view God and themselves, for instance. If you were one of those early followers of Jesus, like the Apostle John, who heard with your own ears the prayers of Jesus how would you view God? What characteristics or roles of God did Jesus emphasize?

John the Beloved paid close attention to the content of Jesus' prayers. He actually records the longest prayer of Jesus in the bible. The "Son of Thunder" is the only gospel writer to record this prayer of Jesus, and I believe it is crucial to having confidence in our own life of prayer and in our ability in growing mature sons and daughters in the faith.

Everyone prays with greater resolve when they know they are being heard. You know you are being heard in prayer when you approach Yahweh as Jesus did. When we speak of God today, we may dial-in with emphasis on many aspects of His character and nature. But according to Jesus' prayer in John 17, He committed to declare with emphasis God's role as a dedicated Father who makes things right. This is the identity of God as emphasized by Jesus in His prayers, it is how he produced dedicated disciples, and it should be preached, taught, prayed, and sang continually; Yahweh is Father.

## WHEN JESUS PRAYS

John 17 is a public prayer of Jesus' that was meant for His disciples to hear. In this prayer, John records Jesus speaking to the Father in the same manner that He instructed His disciples to speak to God, as Father. In this short time of prayer He references God as Father six times (verses 1, 5, 11, 21, 24, 25). At the end of this prayer, Jesus prays things that absolutely blow my mind. He prays that His disciples will experience love from the Father in the same way He has. He also prays that His disciples would return love to the Father the way He does. And all of this is possible, according to Jesus in this prayer, because He has declared to them the Father's name (God's identity as Father) and because He commits to continue declaring it.

What is even crazier still is this; Jesus' prayers always get answered. Want to remove unbelief and have confidence in prayer? Receive the "Abba" revelation, and pray as Jesus prayed. I'm not talking about a mental recognition that one of God's roles is a Father. I'm talking about it being real to you that God is your Father, moment by moment.

*O righteous Father! The world has not known You, but I have known You; and these have known that You sent Me. And I have declared to them Your name (your identity as a loving and righteous Father), and will declare it, that the love with which You loved Me may be in them, and I in them (John 17:25-26).*

How do we know that "God as Father" is real to us? You know it's real when it's disruptive. When Jesus prays He is certainly disrupting religious sensitivities and misguided views of God. When He prayed, *"O righteous Father! The world has not known You..."* (25), He was not saying that the generation He faced didn't have ideas about God, but that they didn't know Him as Jesus did, in His identity as a loving and righteous Father, and their lives demonstrated this. Their beliefs about God were misguided which led to misguided behavior and misguided prayer (we see this in the various religious groups in the New Testament).

Behaviors stem from our beliefs. If our beliefs about God are inconsistent with the way Jesus declared in the New Testament (primarily as a Holy Father), we get into all kinds of error. But if we get it right, we have clarity and confidence in our identity as Sons, realizing our worth, inheritance, and authority in Christ. But first comes the disruption.

Encountering God as Father will disrupt religious sensitivities of others and our own. It seems too good to be true to us that God is an involved Father and that we really are significant to Him. We can't hold on to rejection when our son-ship is real to us. When it's real to you that Yahweh is your involved Father, there is no more room in your life for faking. Religious games are not even on your radar. You have no one to impress, because your confidence is in your Father and in your son-ship to Him. You feel no need to vindicate yourself, because Father is watching. Dad is pleased with you, so there is no need to get caught up in the business of "religious sales," bartering to convince people of your worth. You are accepted on the basis of your faith in Jesus alone, and as such, you avoid the open grave of man pleasing. The religious fakers will never understand why you don't do more. As a son, you understand that you don't have to do anything more or anything less than your Father's will.

The religious Pharisees opposed Jesus because of His emphasis on God's role as a personal Father who was pleased with him. This misunderstanding threw the Pharisees' entire system of belief off and led them into a maddening desire to kill Jesus. God's role as an involved Father and your reality as an accepted son will always disrupt the religious order of the day.

> *Therefore the Jews sought all the more to kill Him, because He not only broke the Sabbath, but also said that God was His Father, making Himself equal with God (John 5:18).*

Many think that God is mostly sad and mad, especially when we sin. But when we get the "Abba" revelation as Jesus had, we run to the Father when we sin and not from Him. When your son-ship is real you no longer put yourself in punishment. Instead, you run to the Father's embrace and away from sin, just like the Prodigal Son. I believe that the key to disrupting the religious spirit is connecting people to God as Father. This not only makes us real sons, but also empowers us to grow other real sons and daughters.

## GROWING DEVOTED DISCIPLES
## FILLED WITH WONDER

In John 17, Jesus makes a strong prayer of commitment to God the Father. He commits to make dedicated disciples by declaring with emphasis God's role as Father. He said, *"Father, I have declared to them Your name, and will declare it"* (John 17).

This is how Jesus made lovesick worshippers, not by focusing entirely upon behaviors, but by addressing their beliefs about God. Even though the world didn't understand God in this way, Jesus committed to declare the Father's name, knowing that this "Abba" revelation would produce disciples after His likeness.

It worked. The evidence is overwhelming. The New Testament reveals that the disciples of Jesus did indeed get Jesus' message of God as Father. Every New Testament Epistle but three begins with a reference to God as Father, and two out of those three have references to the Father within the first few paragraphs. The only New Testament Epistle that doesn't reference the Father is 3 John. This is a much different emphasis on God's role than what's revealed in the Old Testament. Jesus' disciples got the message because Jesus committed to declare, with emphasis, God as Father. If we commit to declare with emphasis God's role as Father, we will have lovesick disciples of Jesus strengthened in the face of temptation, confident in their calling, and willing to hand over everything to God. Here is a quick list of pointers in the Gospels that the disciple's embraced Jesus' pattern to emphasize that God is Father:

References to God as Father in the Gospels:

- Matthew – 43 references to God as Father
- Mark – 5 references to God as Father
- Luke – 14 references to God as Father
- John – 115 references to God as Father.

With just a quick glance over this list it is clear that John, the Son of Thunder ran with the "Abba" revelation with over 115 references to God as Father. John was the only disciple that bravely stood by Jesus at cross when all others fled. I believe John's dedication is directly linked to the prayer he recorded in John 17. He is expressing his love for God in the way that God loves God. I'm right here. Not moving. Dedicated. His son-ship to God was real.

## RECEIVE THE CHARGE

### *Three Ways to Make Our Son-Ship Real*

God wants this revelation to be living understanding for us moment by moment. In order for us to live from this place of knowing God as Father, I believe there are some helpful pointers along the journey that we need to keep in mind:

1. **Fathers make sons. Sons do not make fathers.**
It is one thing to have head knowledge that God is a Father; it is quite another thing to have God Himself make this revelation heart-knowledge, making it real to you. You are not the Father, so you can't make this real to yourself, the Father will as you yield to the Holy Spirit and appropriate faith in Jesus' prayer for you. You do this by renewing your mind in those passages of scripture that speak to this truth. Jesus declares to us God's role as Father so that we may experience the same love that He shares as a Son.

*And I have declared to them Your* name (your identity as a loving and righteous Father), *and will declare it, that the love with which You loved Me may be in them, and I in them* (John 17:26).

2. **Talk to the Holy Spirit.** Experiencing this same love happens again and again by the ministry of Holy Spirit. The Spirit continually leads us into the reality that we are children of God. He awakens and confirms the experience of Sons. If we want to have sustained conversation with God, it must be real to us that we are His children. This is vital to having confidence in prayer and growing disciples. Many people view God as a tyrannical dictator who is impossible to please. Therefore, they only hear condemning blows of accusation, and they think it's God. To know that we are children of God is more than a concept. It takes the Holy Spirit to

lead us into our identity as a "son" (child of God). Truly, *"For as many as are led* (present participle – continually being led) *by the Spirit of God, these are sons of God" (Rom. 8:14).* It's a reality, and it takes the Holy Spirit as our witness to make our adoption real moment by moment.

*The Spirit Himself bears witness with our spirit that we are children of God* (Romans 8:16).
*For as many as are led by the Spirit of God, these are sons of God* (Romans 8:14).

3. **Talk to God as an Involved Father.** It is by the Spirit of Adoption that we can truly cry out "Abba Father." Abba is a personal name for a father. It is the language of a child who truly knows God as Dad. The Holy Spirit makes the "Abba" revelation real to us. We know his voice and He knows ours because we are children. If the language that the Holy Spirit gives us to use when we talk to God is one of a "Personal Father," then the language that the Father will use to speak with us is that of a "personal son" (child). Because of our faith in Jesus, God speaks to us as His very own son (child). *"...but you received the Spirit of adoption by whom we cry out, "Abba, Father." (Rom. 8:15).*

Knowing God as a wonderful and involved Father awakens the desire to know Him even more. The more you know of God the more you want to know. This is the paradox of love. The more you have the more you want. The longer you linger in God's Presence the more you want. In the next chapter, I describe my journey into a ten-day retreat in the Daniel Boone Forest, back into the simple sacred place of longing for more of God's presence. His manifested presence is the fuel for growing wonder in our hearts. Also, on this retreat God gave me a key to unlocking transformation as He highlighted this phrase, "Seek My Presence."

*So it shall be, while My glory passes by, that I will put you in the cleft of the rock, and will cover you with My hand while I pass by (Exodus 33:22) …Now the Lord descended in the cloud and stood with him there, and proclaimed the name of the Lord.*

(EXODUS 34:5)

*O my dove, in the clefts of the rock, In the secret places of the cliff, Let me see your face, Let me hear your voice; For your voice is sweet, And your face is lovely.*

(SONG OF SOLOMON 2:14)

*When You said, "Seek My face," My heart said to You, "Your face, Lord, I will seek.*

(PSALMS 27:8)

# 08.

# SEEK MY PRESENCE

## FUELING A WONDER MOVEMENT

---

I CAN TAKE YOU TO THE SPOT RIGHT in front of the John Wesley statue at Asbury Theological Seminary where I heard the Lord whisper to my heart; "Matt, I'm taking you into the cleft of the rock." It was totally random. I hadn't been meditating on anything like that. I hadn't recently heard a song with that line in it. I wasn't at all sure what that meant, except to say that I knew it was a reference to scripture, and even though I was in seminary, I probably couldn't have told you off hand where it was. I simply responded with a grin and a "thank you Jesus." I put it on the back burner of my heart.

Two weeks went by and I was leading a team of bible readers at a Bible Reading Marathon in our state capitol.

The marathon consisted of several churches coming together to read the bible from Genesis to Revelation, verse-by-verse, out-loud in public. Each group signed up for different times to read. I had several participants scheduled to cover our time slots, so I left myself open as a floater to be on call in case someone couldn't make their slot.

The first day of the marathon I had a participant cancel just minutes before their scheduled time to read. I got in the car and grumbled my way towards the capitol. I didn't know I was being set up. I walked into the capitol and stepped up to the podium to begin reading the bible where the last group had left off. The bible had a note next to it; "Begin reading here at Exodus 33:22. My sad countenance instantly lightened up as I began to inch my way through this verse; "*So it shall be, while My glory passes by, that I will put you in the cleft of the rock, and will cover you with My hand while I pass by.*" The whisper in front of Wesley's statue was now becoming louder.

I went home meditating on that verse. Two days went by and another participant has to cancel. I had a little better attitude this time, so I put some jams on in the car and sang my way towards the capitol. I walked up to the podium to find out where the last reader left off, "Begin reading here at Song of Solomon 2:14." I began to read, "*O my dove, in the clefts of the rock, In the secret places of the cliff, Let me see your face, Let me hear your voice; For your voice is sweet, And your face is lovely."* I started laughing, trying to read and rejoice at the same time. This is crazy. I couldn't figure out what was going on. Now the whisper had become a shout.

Several months went by, and I felt the need to spend ten days alone with God to pray and write. I reasoned that if I were to lead others into an "Upper Room" culture, then I need to find out what it was like to continue in prayer for ten days just as those disciples did in Acts 1. I let a few friends know about this, and someone spoke up and said, "I know of a retreat in the Daniel Boone forest." I said, "Sounds interesting. What's the name of the retreat?" "It's called CleftRock," they responded. I knew I was being set up, so I immediately arranged a ten-day retreat. I spent a few weeks preparing, having extra family time, fasting and reading everything I could find for motivation to spend ten days alone. The stirring in my heart was hopeful to see why the Lord was calling me into the cleft.

All I did the first day of the retreat was repent. The gentle conviction of the Holy Spirit was leading me down a trail I hadn't expected. Going into this ten days I thought everything was good. I knew I needed to pray and write, but I didn't see how my life had become a complex puzzle with pieces scattered everywhere. The props were coming out from under me. The first two days were an exposure of all of the extra stuff I had made life. I was making my journey back to simple. My prayers of repentance sounded like this: "God, what have I been doing? What have I made this all about? What I really want is Your presence. Show me Your glory."

The next eight days I hiked through the woods, whittled sticks on the front porch, and asked God to intensify the cloud of His presence over my life. I didn't have any immediate breakthrough. Each day as I lingered in God's presence, praying in the Spirit and reading the bible, I became hungrier. Nothing really happened on the surface, but I was recovering my deepest longing, more of His presence. There is probably no greater gift that I needed imparted to me than the gift of hunger for His presence. The Lord was indeed taking me into the cleft of the rock, that place where Moses was taken to when he hungered to see God's glory. *The cleft of the rock is the position of hiding in order to encounter God's glory.* The presence of God is where the gift of hunger is grown. When God's presence becomes heavy it provokes us to become hungry and holy.

The presence of Jesus should be our goal in every spiritual discipline because His presence is the greatest reward. All prayer, fasting, bible study, serving and worship, should be aimed at connecting us to Jesus and to His likeness. Getting us in the presence of Jesus must be the destination of spiritual discipline. This is why we are told to seek His face. The Biblical imagery associated with the "face" of God actually means "God Himself, God's presence" or "His glory in fullness" (Exodus 33:20). So, to "seek God's face" is to seek God Himself, His presence, or His glory in fullness.

The Hebrew expression "face" means "before," or "in front of," (Mt. 11:10; Mk 1:2). To be invited to "see the face" is to gain acceptance into someone's presence (Gen. 32:20; Esther 1:14). The face of Moses was shinning, because he had been in the presence (before the face) of God (Ex 34:29; 2 Cor 3:7). Then there are those, in the bible that want to live in the presence of God, obeying his command "Seek my face" (Ps 27:8). Again, seeking God's face is to seek His Presence, it has the same implied pursuit.

I love passages of the bible that give me a clear remedy. 2 Chronicles 7:14 is one of the clearest remedies for us to apply when we are in desperation for God to hear us from heaven, forgive our sin, and heal our land. Every phrase is vital to the solution, but I think the Holy Spirit is highlighting the words, "seek My face" in 2 Chronicles 7:14 today. God is calling us to seek His glory in fullness.

> *Then the Lord appeared to Solomon by night, and said to him: I have heard your prayer, and have chosen this place for Myself as a house of sacrifice. When I shut up heaven and there is no rain, or command the locusts to devour the land, or send pestilence among My people, if My people who are called by My name will humble themselves, and pray and seek My face, and turn from their wicked ways,*

*then I will hear from heaven, and will forgive their sin and heal their land (2 Chronicles 7:13-14).*

It is important to remember that this remedy is given to Solomon during an encounter with the Lord's manifested presence. The Lord appeared to Solomon to give him the prescription for answered prayer, forgiven sins, and a healed land. Also, the Lord's charge to seek His face in this passage would've reminded Solomon of his father David and his passionate pursuit of the presence of God. In fact, the Lord means to do exactly that, to highlight "seeking His face" as a main goal in this verse and to connect Solomon and the people to pursue His presence like David. I say this because the next verses call us right back to seeing aspects of the Lord's face, *"Now **My eyes** will be open and **My ears** attentive to prayer made in this place... **My eyes** and My heart will be there perpetually"* (15, 16).

There is no use to speak of prayer if there are no "eyes" and "ears" of the Lord to see and hear it. Which tells me that our prayer meetings should first be "presence meetings." 2 Chronicles 7 gets better, in the next verse the Lord charges Solomon; *"walk before Me as your father David walked..."* (17). It as if the Lord is reminding Solomon of his father David's pursuit of God's presence and that this would be the major key to answered prayer. I believe the Lord is taking out His highlighter, wanting to mark up every place in our bibles and in our songs that call us to be before Him, to seek His face, His presence. He's invading our prayer rooms, our worship gatherings and our prayer closets with this burning desire of His, "seek My face, My presence, and My glory in fullness."

## RALLY AROUND THE PRESENCE OF JESUS

With the presence of Jesus at the centerpiece of body life, we will begin to make disciples of nations in the presence of God. Where we rally not around sermons and songs and prayers, but around the presence of Jesus. We will certainly teach, sing, and pray the Word, but with the faith to do this in the presence of the Living Word.

In 2 Chronicles 7:12-14, the Lord promises to hear, forgive, and heal when the people follow the prescriptions (stipulations) of humbling themselves, praying, seeking God's face, and repenting. God wants to open the doors of heaven, but they hinge upon this "If my people..." If they follow the prescription, it will position them to receive the cure, which is open heavens, answered prayer, and breakthrough from God. The ball is in our court, it's our move, "If my people..."

In 2 Chronicles 6, Solomon asked God for help when the people sinned. God responds to Solomon with a prescription for restoration. The key to receiving restoration of rain, healing, and provision is to follow the prescription *God's* way.

## THE PRESCRIPTION

Prescription #1 – "Humble Yourself"

Prescription #2 – "Pray"

Prescription #3 – *"Seek My Face/Presence"*

Prescription #4 - "Turn and Trust"

## THE CURE

God Hearing from Heaven

God Forgiving Our Sin

God Healing Our Land

I think a key to unlocking 2 Chronicles 7:14 is understanding that the Lord is in control of the Heavens. *Notice the many references in the passage the Lord makes to himself – "I", "My", "Myself" – indicating with emphasis that He is the one who shuts heaven and he is the one who opens heaven.* The enemy is in not control of the heavens. He may try to trespass over cities and nations, but we have authority to remove his influence in Jesus name. Our enemy may have influence over nations and cities but he is not in control. Other people are not in control of the heavens. Our God is in control, and He will release the breakthrough when we meet His prescriptions (stipulations). God must be sought God's way.

In the OT, it is common to find a reference to God as the Lord of Hosts. The Lord of Hosts is a reference to God's lordship (sovereign control) over the heavens, the realm of the spirit, and the angel armies. *Since the Lord is control of the heavens the only way to receive healing for the land is to do it His way.* The healing of our land is not going to happen because of more "do-gooder" activity, more philanthropy, and more soup kitchens. Working for justice is great, but if it is not borne from the place of intercession, it will not heal the land. Healing of the land only comes from Heaven. No amount of human activity can make us any better. The course of history is in the hands of those who will humble themselves and pray.

Once we understand that God is in control of the heavens and that we must seek God on God's terms, we must realize that we have a role to play. We cannot just "punt" to God's providence and think that it will just happen "if" God wants it to. The cure that God wants to release hinges entirely upon our response. Our response with humility, prayer, seeking His presence, and repentance is an expression of meeting God's stipulation, then God moves. It's Heaven's Blank Check; to the extent you obey I will answer, forgive, and heal. Many fail to realize this simple truth because they do understand intercession as a real partnership with God. They say, "God can do whatever He wants, and there is nothing we can do about it." That's a half-truth. God is not some abstract concept. God is a loving Father wanting us to pray and to commune with him about our need.

## RECEIVE THE CHARGE

We must seek God on God's terms. Take His prescription for answered prayer, forgiveness of sin, and healing of our land. Today, I believe that the Lord is highlighting, "Seek My Face," as a vital part of this charge of humbling ourselves, praying, and turning from darkness. God is orchestrating a global Presence Movement fueled by wonder.

## THE PRESCRIPTION

**Prescription #1 – Humble yourself.** How do you humble yourself? A great way to express humility is by setting apart time for corporate fasting and repentance. Vocalize your dependence upon God for everything. Humility involves dependency upon God and agreeing with the truth. Vocalize in prayer that you need God and that you agree with what His word declares.

**Prescription #2 – Pray.** Pray with a mandate to open up the heavens. The context of this verse describes a people charged by God to pray because the heavens over them are shut and there is no rain. Pray with faith to see heaven open. Fill your heart and your prayer meetings with faith building scriptures. Recall bible stories where God has answered prayer. Pray with every manner of prayer corporately and privately. Pray earnestly and persistently. Lift up your voice and call upon God. Commit to pray until the heavens are open or the answers come.

**Prescription #3 – "Seek My Face/Presence"** by pursuing God's glory in worship. Go after Him and not just an answer. Meditate on His face. Pray as though He is standing in front of you. Sing as though He alone hears you.

**Prescription #4 - "Turn and Trust"** through repentance. Ask God to forgive you and then break any agreement with the lies of the enemy. Be bold enough to expose wickedness in your heart. Ask the Holy Spirit to reveal any wicked way in you. Turn from that wickedness and pursue God's forgiveness.

## THE CURE

**God Hearing from Heaven –** God will demonstrate that He hears our prayer.

**God Forgiving Our Sin –** After we repent we must receive forgiveness. That may sound simple but it's a vital part of the cure. Receiving forgiveness can be harder than repenting.

**God Healing Our Land –** Open heavens always impact the land. God's justice comes to our streets, people get saved, crime goes down, and resources abound.

———

*"Disturb us, Lord, to dare more boldly,*
*To venture on wilder seas*
*Where storms will show Your mastery;*
*Where losing sight of land,*
*We shall find the stars."*

SIR FRANCIS DRAKE

———

## 09.

# NEW CLOUDS OF UNKNOWING

ENTERING ATMOSPHERES
HIGHER THAN KNOWING GOD

---

"WHAT IS YOUR DREAM?" That was the question my Christian Ethics professor challenged us with in undergrad. He went on to ask, "What is it that you strive for? Before you answer this question, I want you to try and think of a target that you could aim for all the days of your life. Tell us what you could spend your whole life pursuing and never fully exhaust. You could attain it, but still there would be more to attain. You could do this everyday. Now, I want each of you to come up to the marker board and fill in this blank: I strive to _____."

I knew exactly what I wanted to write in that blank. All my life I've heard messages and read books about someone else's devotion to Jesus. I wanted to know God like they did. They knew God in ways that were real to them. This is the reason I went to Bible College, and it was the reason I daily pursued God in prayer and study. I strived to know God. I could hardly wait my turn to run up to the marker board and impress the class with my awesome dream to know God. I didn't realize that my dream was about to get an upgrade.

Several students went to the marker board and wrote things like, "I strive to please God," or "I strive to be successful." Then my turn came. In my arrogance, I was anxious to erase their low-level dreams and blast them with my brilliance. I strutted up to the marker board and with a big smirk on my face wrote, "I strive to <u>know God</u>." I put the marker down and walked back to my seat like I did something special. The Professor looked at my statement and said, "Wow, Matt. You've nailed it on the head. You could always be pursing the knowledge of God. Always growing in your understanding of God. It's immeasurable. I really like that."

Then my Professor walked over to his seat and just sat there quietly looking at the marker board. Then he looked at me and said, "But is there anything higher? Is there anything higher than pursuing the knowledge of God?" I said, "No sir. Jesus said that the knowledge of God is eternal life. Jeremiah wrote that a man can't glory in wisdom, strength, or riches, but he can glory in the knowledge of God. And Daniel, he said that if we know God we'll be strong and do great exploits." The Professor said, "That is all true Matt. And you are right. But is there a higher dream to pursue than knowing God?" Then he walked over to the marker board and said, "What if I erase your word 'know' here and replace it with the word 'love?' So, now it reads, 'I strive to love God.'"

If I were a cartoon character you could've seen a huge light bulb over my head after he said that. Now, obviously you've got to know God in order to love Him. However, loving Him is a higher dream. In all your searching, seeking, knocking and pursuing do not forget to pause and to stand in awe of the God who is pursuing you in love. This is vital to prayer. This is vital to our sense of wonder. More than figuring Him out, we need opportunities to just hang out with God and linger in His presence.

## CHEW YOUR ORTHODOXY

Loving God is a higher focus for our devotional life than trying to know God. I'm not just reading my bible or praying to figure God out or to figure a situation out. I want to slip from desk and into the pages. I read my bible to encounter Jesus and to express my attachment to Him. For years, I've studied the knowledge of God in Bible College, Seminary, and preparing lessons for theology classes that I'm teaching, and I'm still determined to provoke my generation to pursue the knowledge of God. We must disciple people in the knowledge of God. But this is not all. The knowledge of God must be set ablaze by the love of God. Otherwise, we just become people watching the show, and we never get on the journey of truly walking with God. If we are not wise to raise knowledge to the level of love and worship of Jesus, we could become guilty of Maximus the Confessor's warning, *"Theology without action is the theology of demons."*

After years of studying the knowledge of God, I've found that I don't really "get it" until my understanding of God evokes worship and wonder. I can say that I grasp the omniscience of God, that I understand that God knows everything, and there isn't anything that He doesn't know. But it's a whole a different level of conversation to say that it is real to me that God knows my rising and my sitting, that He knows me perfectly, and His thoughts are always on me, and He's never distracted from me.

All orthodoxy (right belief) must evoke wonder and worship. Demons know the scriptures, they even believe that Jesus rose from the dead, but they are not saved; they are not worshipping God. It's not enough to have your study of the end times teased out in perfect graphs and charts; you've got to live a life in view of eternity everyday.

Many people miss out on a more accurate way because of their familiarity with what they know. Knowledge never takes that eighteen-inch drop from their heads to their hearts. For fools, knowledge never becomes wisdom. When God begins to grind to powder what was once simple head knowledge and says, "Eat this," it's time to just swallow! Chew your orthodoxy. Meditate on those truths until they are digested and become a part of you. Allow right beliefs in your head to spark wonder and worship in your hearts. Turn truth into prayers. Are we willing to allow the Holy Spirit to make the truths of the bible a reality to us? I am talking about God making truths of the bible real to your own heart, knowing things by revelation, and not just with your grey matter.

You're a person of great understanding when you realize that you don't have it all figured out. Jesus said that when you come into a room you're supposed to take the lowest seat in the house. We esteem others by realizing that we can learn from everyone. The bible even speaks of learning from ants! A disciple of Jesus is an apprentice of Jesus. Disciples are learners, those who take upon themselves the teachings of Jesus through his word, his life, and his creation. When a more accurate way is presented to us, are we willing to embrace it? The way of knowledge puffs up, but the way of love humbles and keeps us teachable.

## WISDOM EVOKING WONDER

Every personal renewal in my life came as result of the Holy Spirit making real to me some aspect of the knowledge of God or some aspect of my identity in Jesus. In other words, God made real to me some aspect of Himself or who I am in Him. In essence, knowledge of God led to love of God, worship and wonder. It truly takes the Spirit of wisdom and revelation to move head-knowledge to heart-knowledge. To me, this is vital for discipleship. I can hardly think of a more important thing to talk about in discipleship than helping folks find out who Jesus really is, find out who they really are in Jesus, and find the Holy Spirits' power to make it real to them (Spirit of Wisdom and Revelation). In other words, discipleship must make real to us what we learn. I suggest a discipleship plan that looks like this:

1. Find out who God is (knowledge of God's ways, character, names, etc.)
2. Find out who you are in God (identity in Christ as believers, sons, bride, etc.)
3. Find the Holy Spirit's power to make these truths real to us (Spirit of Wisdom and Revelation, heart-knowledge, experiential knowledge, love of God, etc.)

This model of discipleship bridges the gap between head

knowledge and heart knowledge. The reason that I want to know more about God is because I love Him. The more I know the more I love. What I do not understand yet fully doesn't trip-up my love for Him because figuring Him out is not my primary goal anyway. I'm living with some elements of mystery here. I do not know God fully, but that doesn't mean that I do not know Him truly. I'm not groping around in the dark looking for God. What I do know of Him is real. It is so real, in fact, that it won't leave me alone demanding a response. The response of someone seeking knowledge will be philosophical (love of wisdom), and they walk away with a truth to impress all of their friends. I think the response of a disciple of Jesus to the knowledge of God is love, obedience, worship, reverence and awe. The goal is to let what I know make that 18-inch drop to my heart and cause me to love God. Even what I do not understand evokes worship and love. Knowledge is always supposed to lead us to intimacy with God.

## LOVERS OF GOD ARE WISEST

Think of this, the wisest man in history wrote the most intimate book of the Bible. Lovers of God are wisest. Let me explain. The Proverbs direct us: get wisdom (Wisdom is the principal thing; therefore get wisdom - Proverbs 4:7). We are challenged to get wisdom because God wants to release His secrets, strategies, and practical advice to those who will cultivate intimacy and reverence for Him. We are challenged to get wisdom. But this wisdom is deeply spiritual and livable. Let's consider the connectedness between wisdom and intimacy with God.

First, the wise know and fear God. When I think of a wise person, I have this picture of an older person with grey hair, because I believe that wisdom comes from experience. And it's true, experience does lead to wisdom. But in the biblical world, wisdom didn't come from experience primarily. You were wise to the extent that you knew (through experiential knowledge) and feared (reverenced) God. You could be 18 years old and full of Godly wisdom because you demonstrated a love for God with holy fear. Biblical wisdom comes from being close to the heart of God, from fellowship, from intimacy with God, and from making decisions that honor His Lordship. As Proverbs 9:10 has shown, "The fear of the LORD is the beginning of wisdom, And the knowledge of the Holy One is understanding." This "knowledge of the Holy One" is revelation gained by encounter. This is how wisdom leads to wonder, because true information has been made real to you by encountering the Holy Spirit. Knowing God is glorious, but the path to knowing God begins with fearsome wonder. As Proverbs 1:7 makes clear, "The fear of the LORD is the beginning of knowledge, But fools despise wisdom and instruction."

Secondly, wisdom flows from intimacy with God. We must keep in front of us the fact that *the wisest man in history wrote the most intimate book of the bible.* The Old Testament has a clear picture of wisdom coming from intimacy with God, its called "The Song of All Songs" or "The Song of Solomon." It was said that Solomon "...*was wiser than all men... and his fame was in all the surrounding nations*"(I Kings 4:31). Just like Job, Proverbs, Ecclesiastes, and some of the Psalms, the Song of Solomon is in the category of Hebrew Wisdom Literature. It is a picture of Godly decision-making that springs from a love covenant between Solomon and his bride. It is called "The Song of all Songs." *It is as if Solomon is saying with this Song, "to love God and be loved by him is the best decision I ever made. I was most-wise when I wrote the "Song of Solomon."*

Before Solomon was God's wise man, he was God's dearly loved. In 2 Sam. 12:24-25, God had even given Solomon another name before he was even born, he called him Jedidiah (beloved of the Lord). It was said that "*Solomon loved the LORD, walking in the statutes of his father David*" (I Kings 3:3). Wisdom, godly-decision making, and walking in the Kingdom dimension of wisdom all spring from wonder-filled intimacy with God.

To be clear, we cannot love God without knowing Him. I'm simply saying that loving God is a higher goal and more worthy pursuit. Love is the finish line of devotion. Get wisdom (knowledge of God gained by encounter). Allow what knowledge you gain to make that drop from your head to your heart. Be a bible nerd. But allow your bible "nerdery" to turn you into a wonder-filled worshipper. Head knowledge must awaken a holy heart or it's incomplete. Make love your aim. Allow wisdom to evoke wonder. Chew your orthodoxy.

## RECEIVE THE CHARGE

### *Ways to Walk in "Wonder Evoking Wisdom"*

1. **Make Love Your Aim:** Let every spiritual discipline you engage in have the goal to connect you to Jesus and to His likeness.

2. **Study the Bible in Community:** We all must study the bible in the secret place with God. It also very helpful to study in groups, or at least have a sounding board with others to share the truths you are discovering. Studying in community helps connect knowledge to real life. Our discoveries can move from head to heart as we hear truth come alive in others. There is something about the preached Word or the spoken Word in a group that ignites faith and worship.

3. **Meditate on Truths Until They Touch Your Heart:**
Meditating on Scriptures is a powerful way to connect head knowledge to heart knowledge. Turn truths into prayers and songs. Praying the scriptures or thinking on them throughout the day are helpful ways to digest truth and make it apart of us. Praying the Bible is a helpful link to move you from a "hearer" only to a "doer" of the word. This gives bible study a goal: to connect with God in prayer and to become obedient and Christlike. We are seeking to have a Word-Shaped life and not just mental assents to propositional truth claims.

---

*"Is not this a brand plucked out of the fire?"*

(ZECHARIAH. 3:2)

---

# 10.

# STRIKE
# THE GROUND

## RELEASING WONDER TO OTHERS

———

HAVING BEEN MARKED BY GOD's majestic glory at the throne, we are then hurled into all the earth to release His glory to others. In prayer and devotion we have stood before The Lord and allowed His lightning to melt our hearts again. Wonder has made us fully alive to God and at war with sin. We are ready to fuel a wonder movement. Now that we've received a wonder-filled heart in the secret place, we are now ready to release wonder to others. Released from the cloud, we strike the ground as intercessors invoking God's will with authority: "On earth as it is in heaven."

Nothing we encounter is more real than the place we just came from. We've been breathing rarified air, have felt the cool winds of eternity in our secret place with God, and are ready to make the transition into all the earth. We are in the world but not of it. We have gone up, found keys in those clouds and have returned to unlock doors here that no man can close and to close doors no man can open. Some have keys of authority to impact the church, government, media, families, or other spheres of the culture. Others strike the ground calling everyone to build God a dwelling place in every city. Still some exit the cloud and immediately pioneer trails of evangelism in places where the gospel has not been. Having been with Jesus we are taking His message and wonder to the slums, garbage heaps, hospitals, marketplaces… wherever He'll send us. We are living from the cloud. Living from a burning place with God. We have received wonder and now it is time to release wonder.

## LIVING FROM THE BURNING

There is an example from history that I believe highlights the journey from receiving wonder to releasing it others. When John Wesley was five years old, he nearly lost his life when his family's home caught on fire in the middle of the night. All the children made it safely out of the house, but when they were counted, John was still missing. A farmer from nearby saw John in an upstairs window surrounded by the leaping flames. Several neighbors made a "human ladder" by climbing on each other's shoulders, until the man on top was able to grab John and pull him out of the burning home. Shortly after he was rescued, the entire house exploded in flames. He barely escaped alive.

From this experience and for the rest of his life, John Wesley referred to himself "as a brand plucked from the burning," quoting Zechariah 3:2. In fact, the experience so defined Wesley that when he wrote his own epitaph, he required that his gravestone read; "Here lieth the body of John Wesley, a brand plucked from the burning." That is all that he wanted to be remembered as; a burning man. He spent His life releasing a burning zeal for the Lord to others.

Indeed, Wesley had been delivered from the fire so that God might be glorified in him. He grew to become an Anglican cleric and Christian theologian at Oxford. John and his brother Charles Wesley are mostly known for founding the Methodist movement that began with an emphasis on evangelism, spiritual discipline, and holiness during a time of religious apathy in the Anglican Church.

As a zealous firebrand, Wesley decided to become a missionary and sail to America to impact the First Nations people in Georgia. At one point in the voyage across the Atlantic a storm came up and broke the mast off the ship.

While Wesley panicked in fear for his life, the German Moravians on board calmly sang hymns and prayed. Wesley soon discovered that the Moravians had something that he didn't. He wanted to find out what it was.

After returning to England, on May 24, 1738 he attended a Moravian meeting in Aldersgate Street, London, in which he heard a reading of Luther's preface to the book of Romans. He listened intently to the message of faith being given by the Moravians, and something began to ignite in Wesley. While listening he said, "I felt my heart strangely warmed." This melting of heart in the presence of God revolutionized Wesley's life.

How did the Moravians get such wonder-filled hearts that they could sing in the face of death? The Moravians received wonder by living in a praying community. This praying community shared this wonder with Wesley and they sent missionaries around the world.

Perhaps the greatest story of wonder sharing in history has inspired many for over the last 250 years. The Moravian community aptly named "Hernhutt" (The Lord's Watch) established a 24-hour prayer vigil that lasted over 100 years. The result of this unceasing prayer was a missions movement that embraced the toughest of assignments.

In December 1732, Leonard Dober and David Nitschmann (both in their early twenties) were sent out as the first two Moravian missionaries from this movement.

They departed from Herrnhut, Germany for St. Thomas Island in the West Indies. They sold themselves into slavery to reach 3,000 slaves who worked the sugarcane fields owned by an atheist landowner. The landowner vowed to never allow Christianity to reach his property. Their families, knowing they would never see them again, wept and asked them why they had to go as they departed from Hamburg to sail through the North Sea. One of them cried out what became the banner call for all Moravian missionaries: "May the Lamb that was slain receive the reward of His suffering." The Moravians had a wonderful message to share.

Over the next 150 years, the Moravians sent out 2,000 missionaries to neglected areas of the earth. These are the people that sparked wonder in Wesley's heart. They positioned themselves in prayer and came out in power.

From this marking Wesley began to share wonder. His message was certainly focused on the internal "burning" of the human heart by the grace of God, but he also challenged Christians to live out experientially what they had internally. He fed the poor, worked for prison reform, provided medical aid, and built orphanages.

In his pamphlet "Thoughts Upon Slavery," Wesley challenged slavery and supported the abolition movement. For years William Wilberforce pushed Britain's Parliament to abolish slavery. Discouraged, he was about to give up. His elderly friend, John Wesley heard of it and from his deathbed called for pen and paper. With trembling hand, Wesley wrote:

> "Unless God has raised you up for this very thing, you will be worn out by the opposition of men and devils. But if God be for you, who can be against you? Are all of them stronger than God? Oh be not weary of well-doing! Go on, in the name of God and in the power of his might, till even American slavery shall vanish away before it."

Wesley died six days later, on March 2, 1791, but Wilberforce went on to fight forty-five more years, and in 1833, three days before his own death, saw slavery abolished in Britain. This is what it means to be a brand pulled from the fire of God's presence and sent to change the world.

Wesley's influence of personal holiness has impacted every part of the globe. You can find denominations, movements, and organizations all over the world that are influenced by John Wesley. All of this impact from one firebrand marked by the God of Holy Love.

## SECRET PLACES TO PUBLIC PLACES

Reading Wesley's story makes me appreciate the 100 year

prayer meeting of the Moravians. Without them there would be no Wesley. I think the Moravians discovered something. They prayed up a storm cloud in Herrnhutt that launched bold witnesses to impact others with a burning heart.

The Moravians understood that there are some breakthroughs that will only happen as a result of an assembly at prayer. Jesus promised that the gates of Hell would not be able to stand against the force of an assembly of saints advancing the Kingdom of God under His leadership.

It is also true that some breakthroughs will only be released through private prayer. Jesus promised that open rewards would only come when we enter our closet, shut the door, and pray to the Father in secret. The Father who sees in secret will reward us openly (Matthew 6). Therefore, the Father's open reward only comes from behind a shut door in private prayer. We need an emphasis on both private and public prayer without neglecting the one for the other.

When believers possess a vibrant prayer-life privately, our corporate gatherings for prayer can be much more fruitful. It is not safe to make corporate times of prayer our only time of prayer. We cannot use corporate prayer to get caught up on our private devotional fellowship with God. A solemn assembly will never grant that which God ordained to be given from private prayer. This is one of the biggest causes of burnout when it comes to prayer meetings. When we use corporate prayer alone for our intimacy with God we will rarely contend for answered prayer. Why? Because loving God and being loved by God is primary, and if we are not engaging God's love in private fellowship, there will be no open reward in public prayer.

We won't have any steam to contend in the assembly when the private devotional flame is low. I believe corporate prayer is most fruitful when each of us shows up with an open and public reward from the Father granted to us in the secret place. This is why I believe private prayer is primary. Corporate prayer is a necessary consequence of private devotion. If we only do corporate prayer we will not approach the gathering with an expectation to breakthrough simply because we are using this time to build faith, catch up on intimacy, and get oil for our lamps.

When we descend from the cloud of being alone with God we come to the community with oil already in our lamps and tenderness in our hearts. When we live from the burning place of His presence, found in solitude with God, we become ready to crash Hell's gate and release breakthrough.

## MAKING SOLEMN
## ASSEMBLIES SOLEMN

The key to having awesome worship and prayer meetings is to have even better private ones. Having a private devotional flame before God is the way God has ordained for us to make the solemn assembly "solemn" and to make worship gatherings soar higher. Answered corporate prayer and the release of God's glory is first the result of an individual saint's burning in a secret place with Jesus. The corporate release of authority is first a private reward of abandonment to God alone. The battle is won or lost in the cloud before we show up on earth to the assembly.

The Moravian's didn't need to get the masses on fire for God, but they themselves needed to catch flame in secret places, and bring that out in the open to receive the Father's open reward. It starts with an individual, then a few, then a community, then a region, and so on. A coming outpouring or breakthrough is first a whisper to a person alone with God. They take that sound to others. We want the masses immersed in God. That's the goal. It starts with an individual.

In Section One, we've emphasized how we can position ourselves to receive a wonder-filled heart. In Section Two, we will emphasize how we can experience and release wonder in community, as the Moravians did for Wesley, as Wesley did for the world.

## RECEIVE THE CHARGE

The way we have a release of Kingdom authority corporately is to first have it cultivated in our own personal devotional lives. Strengthening private devotion to Jesus enables us to cultivate an ear to hear, and then we come together to release what we've heard in the secret place. In other words, we hit the ground running, and we strike the ground with impact. Whenever I'm closest to God, I always walk from that encounter with a desire to call people to solemn assemblies. I want others to experience this wonder. I want to encounter corporate wonder. This may be a personal call, but it's exactly what I feel. From the cloud I have a holy jealousy to call people to the Upper Room.

PART TWO

—

# FROM CLOUD TO GROUND: RELEASING WONDER

# 11.

# AGITATED
# BY STORM

## ENCOUNTERING THE MAJESTY OF
## GOD TOGETHER

---

OVER 100 YEARS BEFORE the Azusa Street Revival God invaded the frontier forests of Kentucky. God seemed to be everywhere. It was awful. Wait, I didn't say it was "awesome." No, it was awful, terrifying and scary for the Atheists that visited this place during the awakening. For believers, this place had an awe-inspiring reverential wonder about it. In addition to the awareness of God, there was fiery gospel preaching that would cut men to the heart, awaken them to their need of God, and lead them into a transformed life. History would highlight a blending of prayer, presence, and powerful preaching at Cane

Ridge. I'm actually writing this chapter from a bench inside the prayer house made in 1829 positioned just behind the pulpit dedicated to Barton Stone, who was a leader in the awakening here. It was said that the preaching from this pulpit would go on for days and weeks at a time.

The desperate frontiersmen called this building, "A House of Prayer for all Nations." I love that. The pioneers started with the only proven foundation in history for awakening: prayer. But the prayer culture in this area wasn't the only thing that Cane Ridge was known for. This House of Prayer would soon become a House of God's Presence. There was a strange and unusual awareness of God that saturated the ground here like a Kentucky spring rain. God's weighty presence was here.

I came here today to dream. I'm dreaming of whole communities encountering and sustaining the glory of God. I am imagining these pioneers and their devotional hunger for Jesus, and I am hoping that I can see awakening in my day as they did. I want that awareness of God's presence that lingered here, their sense of wonder. I can just imagine the courage it took to promote Heaven's agenda in such a hopeless area, on the frontier of the bluegrass wilderness. I'm asking the Lord for an impartation, a resolve to see an awakening in my day created in a culture of prayer, with a primary pursuit of seeking God's presence, and power on the preaching of the gospel like they had here.

Cane Ridge was no hype. It was a pioneer's awakening, with pioneer grit, pioneer desperation, and pioneer manifestations. Imagine cutting your way through the forest and being halted in your tracks by distant shouts and screams coming up over the next hill. Then the sound changes to the thunderous preaching of a man doing his best to be heard over the noise of the crowd. He has no microphone, no speakers, no lights, or media. Everything was completely uncomfortable to the seeker and every word born from a burning House of Prayer.

## I WISH I HAD STAYED HOME

In 1801, an atheist named James B. Finley visited the Cane Ridge awakening in Kentucky. James said,

> "*The noise was like the roar of Niagara. The vast sea of human beings seemed to be **agitated as if by a storm**... Some of the people were singing, others praying, some crying for mercy in the most piteous accents, while others were shouting vociferously. While witnessing these scenes, a peculiarly-strange sensation, such as I had never felt before, came over me. My heart beat tumultuously, my knees trembled, my lip quivered, and I felt as though I must fall to the ground. A strange supernatural power*

*seemed to pervade the entire mass of mind there collected. At one time I saw at least 500, swept down in a moment as if a battery of a thousand guns had been opened upon them, and then immediately followed shrieks and shouts that rent the very heavens. I fled for the woods and wished I had stayed at home."*

Dream with me of an awakening in our day so wonderfully awful that the postmodern atheist acknowledges the sheer fierceness of God's nearness. The atheist, James B. Finley wishes he'd stayed home from Cane Ridge meetings because the presence of God he felt here was so real, why do they stay home from our meetings today?

They reported that people shook and lips quivered as others fell to the ground with loud shrieks and shouts. Peter Cartwright was one of the prominent preachers in Cane Ridge. He called the manifestations "the jerks" and said that they seized saints and sinners with convulsive jerking all over, which they could not avoid, and the more they resisted the more they jerked.

## AWAKENING UNTO REFORMATION

The Second Great Awakening (1780-1810) in America was considered great not just because of what it did for the church, but how it transformed culture. It greatly influenced the abolition of slavery, the end of child labor, prompted a move towards literacy for everyone, and called for prison reform. Cane Ridge was so much more than emotional manifestations. It greatly impacted all of society around it. There you have it. What is still the only requirement for a healed society? The glory of God. The only remedy is still, "If my people who are called by my name will humble themselves, and pray and seek My face, and turn from their wicked ways, then I will hear from heaven, and will forgive their sin and heal their land" (2 Chronicles 7:14). We don't do it because it's simple. We don't do it because we have unbelief about prayer.

I am aware that we don't necessarily get to choose the way God brings about change. At Cane Ridge, God chose His presence to be paramount as the instrument of change. His presence only comes to those seeking it. So, I am here today seeking and asking God how we can encounter and release as a community.

## THE HEBRIDES KEY: ARE MY HANDS CLEAN?

As I look up from my laptop here at the Cane Ridge Meeting House, I've noticed that there's an old bible published in

1836 on the pulpit sitting in front of me and its laying open to Psalms 24. Thirty minutes have passed since my last sentence. I've paused from writing to reread Psalms 24 and my inner nerd is giggling like a mad scientist whose light bulb overhead just lit up the room. I haven't thought of it for a long time, but I know from studying history that Psalms 24 happens to be a passage that sparked another great revival in the Hebrides Islands off the coast of Scotland. Maybe the Lord is trying to say something to me.

I remember that they were hungry for God and had been gathering together to pray for months at a time. In one prayer gathering they got a spark from Psalms 24, "Who may ascend into the hill of the Lord? Who may stand in His holy place? He who has clean hands and a pure heart, who has not lifted up his soul to an idol, nor sworn deceitfully."

While reading Psalms 24 one of the young men stood up in that prayer meeting and said, ""It seems to me to be so much humbug to be praying as we are praying, to be waiting as we are waiting, if we ourselves are not right with God." He then lifted up his hands and began to cry out; "God, are my hands clean? Is my heart pure?" The revival was now on, and it changed the whole community. It was reported that God seemed to be everywhere in the Hebrides. Revival spread throughout the islands. The Hebrides experienced communal wonder.

The answer from Heaven came to those on the Hebrides

because they answered the question that would open them up to reverential wonder, "Are my hands clean? Is my heart pure?" They each, individually, became rightly related to God. They each began to take seriously Psalms 24 and to seek God's face, His presence like Jacob (Psalms 24:6).

Today, I believe the Lord is marking a generation with "Psalms-24-honesty," that we all would see the futility of going to meeting after meeting without clean hands, pure hearts, and our own souls purged of idolatry. Getting honest with God would enable us to see the humbug of climbing just for the sake of climbing or praying just to be praying. I want to ascend the hill of the Lord because it's the Lord's hill. I want to climb because His presence is at the top. Let meeting with God be the goal of every gathering. Give a generation, with Jacob-like tenacity, a purpose worth climbing for, His Presence.

## PSALMS 24 HONESTY

"Psalms 24 Honesty" is on this generation. They want what's real. They crave truth without hype, false motive, and exploitation. I'm going to stand in Barton Stone's Pulpit here today at the Cane Ridge Meeting House and declare Psalms 24 as loud as I can. Let the Hebrides Key of authenticity and personal purity unlocks corporate displays of God's power through a governing ecclesia again. Let the Hebrides Key of Psalms 24 Honesty release true worshippers, and let every hidden sin in our hearts be unearthed and brought to Jesus. Let every religious mask be removed, and let every twice-dead microphone be unplugged. God, start with me. Let each of us individually become rightly related to Jesus and share our passion for Him with others

I believe a historic awakening is here upon us that will birth church and societal reform in some fresh ways. God has called many out of common-sense lifestyles and common-sense churches to be reformers. I'm specifically seeing devotional reformers. In the grace of God, they will change the understanding and expression of devotion to Jesus. They will introduce a new normal and a new radical. In fact, they have been rejected by the normal and they need to thank God that they've been rejected. God saved them for awakening and from the Father's discipline that's coming upon the sleeping church. These reformers enjoy devotion, its not a labor, its not to earn something, its simply their joy to burn for God. Let us learn from Cane Ridge. Let us learn from the Hebrides Islands. Let "Psalms 24 honesty" come to an entire generation.

## RECEIVE THE CHARGE

1. After reading this chapter, what stood out to you the most? Ask the Lord why?

2. The Hebrides revival began as a result of "Psalms 24 Honesty." How do you know that you are rightly related to God?

*And when they had entered,
they went up into the
upper room where they
were staying… These all
continued with one accord
in prayer and supplication,
with the women and
Mary the mother of Jesus,
and with His brothers…
(altogether the number of
names was about a hundred
and twenty).*

(ACTS 1:13-15)

# 12.

# RED SKIES
# AT MORNING

## THE SIGNIFICANCE OF THE HOUR CALLS
## FOR UPPER ROOM LIGHTNING

———

"SIGNS AND WONDERS, MIRACULOUS powers, prophecy, healing. Release, release, release," they sang. I was at the "50 State Tour" in Lexington, Kentucky, and I had no idea what I was getting into. I was in grad school, working on my M.A. at Asbury Seminary in Wilmore, Kentucky, when a classmate invited me to come check out this prayer gathering. Shofars, banners, and Star of David necklaces, this was going to be different. I grew up in a Pentecostal, revival-fire atmosphere. We didn't have shofar's and flag wavers. But as soon as worship started and the intercession began to rumble, I felt at home.

The presence of Jesus filled the room and the entire meeting was a conglomerate of prayer, prophecy, and presence. It was on. One particular word shared was by Dutch Sheets. He took the pulpit and said, "The State of Kentucky has 120 counties, so I guess we'll call this an Upper Room State." I had never heard Dutch Sheets speak before; it was the first thing I'd ever heard him say. It stuck with me. It sounded an alarm inside of me. In fact, that whole meeting activated something in me that had been there all along. It was my awakening bones rattling inside. I felt the significance of the hour and had a boldness to blast a trumpet to my generation. I was connecting with a tribe of intercessors, and I believed in that moment that I would be part of an Upper Room Culture of prevailing prayer. I had faith in that moment that I could synergize my prayers with the book of Acts saints for outpouring. It became real to me that I am connected with 120 people that actually prevailed in prayer for an outpouring of the Spirit and shared it with the nations of the earth.

I went home from the meeting and quickly wrote the experience down in my journal. I wanted to capture the feeling you get when you find out who you are, and you're okay with it. The sound being released in that meeting was unveiling who I was and thereby creating my future. It was like connecting with a power-surge of God's providence. I wrote:

"This is what I'm called to. God, don't let this movement of prayer and awakening pass me by. I want your presence. I must have more of you. This has been one of those providential weekends with Your hand all over it. It has a sense of destiny all over it. I feel as though Heaven was taking attendance to make sure I was here."

There's an old saying, "Red skies at morning, Sailors take warning." It's an idea that red skies in the morning are an indication of an approaching storm. That day and every day since, I've been waking up to red skies at morning. I see a storm coming. It's not a bad storm. It's the storm around Yahweh's throne. I feel the significance of the hour and how desperate our times are. I'm putting the trumpet to my mouth to sound an alarm, shutting down business as usual, and entering the Upper Room.

What I heard in that meeting years ago is a major part of everything I do today, establishing an Upper Room Culture of solemn assemblies, laboring in prayer for the fullness of the Spirit, and releasing witnesses for Jesus with power evangelism, and more. I long to see today's disciples pass through the Upper Room gate and come out transforming the culture. I pray, write, and labor for this, but it was first a sound that I heard, "An Upper Room State."

Faith is often a sound first. Faith comes by hearing.

I heard something in that gathering that unlocked faith in me to enter the Upper Room context of perpetual solemn assembly until God releases the breakthrough. In that meeting I listened to them pray and declare. I watched Jesus paint my future with a sound. It was the sound of an alarm.

## WHAT WAS THE UPPER ROOM?
### *A Perpetual Solemn Assembly Until Breakthrough*

In the early 1900's, a young Welsh coal miner named Evan Roberts was gripped by God for revival. He was "bent" by God's burden for the lost and to see his nation awakened. His prayer was that God would shut Hell's gates over his nation for one year and thereby set up a roadblock for those racing towards that place of eternal torment with no exits. His devotion triggered a turning point in redemption history; a revival began that produced the fruit of more than 100,000 conversions.

The Upper Room was exactly that; a prayer meeting that triggered a turning point in redemption history. I am even willing to say that prayer, for Luke (the author of Luke-Acts), not only triggers turning points in redemption history, but also is the very means that God uses to guide redemption history.

From the Ascension of Jesus to the Day of Pentecost

(ten days), 120 disciples of Jesus were gathered together eagerly waiting for the promise of the Holy Spirit; they were commanded by Jesus to tarry in Jerusalem until they received power from on high (Luke 24:49; Acts 1:12-15). They did not decide to pray for ten days. They decided to pray until they were endued with power from on high, it just happened to take ten days. For ten days they wholeheartedly turned to the Lord together with continual prayer until the breakthrough came.

At the ninth hour of the day on the morning of the Feast of Pentecost, a sound like a violent rushing wind filled the Upper Room, and they saw tongues of fire resting on them, and all one hundred twenty were filled with the Spirit as Joel prophesied (Acts 2:1-4). Peter got up and explained what was going on by telling the onlookers that this outpouring of the Holy Spirit was the fulfillment of what was spoken by the prophet Joel; that in the last days God would pour out His Spirit on all flesh (Joel 2:29).

Peter drew a connection between their continual prayer and the outpouring of the Spirit, saying, "…this is what was spoken by the prophet Joel…" (Acts 2:16). Why could Peter say this with such confidence? Because he knew what was going on for ten days in the Upper Room prior to the outpouring was the same thing modeled in Joel that must take place prior to outpouring. Peter knew the manifestations of the Spirit on the Day of Pentecost had to be what Joel prophesied, because the Holy Spirit inspired him to see this and because he knew they were doing what was prescribed by Joel before the outpouring was to come. They had prayed up a storm. Red skies at morning, sailors take warning.

## THE UPPER ROOM PRESCRIPTION

Nothing stirs your heart to pray with authority like knowing that God is watching and listening. Luke the physician means to help us with that when writing the Book of Acts. He was a physician, but he thought like a "prayer evangelist" to a prayer-less church. It is as if he was saying, "I am an eyewitness of the great Physician while I was in pre-med. His remedy to every crisis was prayer." *Luke means to remove our unbelief about prayer and spark faith in our hearts that prayer is the means by which God guided history in the life of Jesus and in the early Church.* This was in the mind of the Upper Room praying church, and it gave them the resolve they needed to continue steadfastly in prayer and supplication.

Luke, as a historian, isn't just *describing* details of the Upper Room. Luke, as a physician, is *prescribing* for us the details of the Upper Room. The Upper Room is not just a description, it's a prescription given to the church of all ages by God through Luke the physician (Col. 4:14). This prescription turns us wholeheartedly to God and triggers turning points in history. How can I be sure that Luke is not just describing events? Two reasons:

1.  ***The Prayer-Thread of Luke-Acts:*** Luke-Acts has a strong prayer-pattern running from beginning to end. Over and over, Luke shows how prayer positions us to encounter God's presence, which triggers His power. For Luke, prayer triggers turning points again and again in Luke-Acts. The Upper Room followed this pattern through unceasing prayer.

2.  ***Joel's Solemn Assembly:*** The Upper Room prayer gathering was patterned after Joel's solemn assembly, which included a wholehearted return to God in prayer. *No one can pray "Fill me" until they've prayed "Empty me."* Joel's solemn assembly is about the prayer of "Empty me." It's about giving ourselves wholeheartedly to the Lord. After our wholehearted response, we are filled with His Spirit.

The Upper Room was a perpetual solemn assembly modeled after God's pattern given in the book of Joel for the outpouring of the Holy Spirit. In the book of Joel, we see that turning to God wholeheartedly through continual prayer evokes God's presence, which enables power evangelism. Joel's solemn assembly was all about coming to God with our whole heart and staying there until God releases the outpouring.

If you are to release corporate wonder you must sound the alarm. You must rally believers to wholehearted assemblies. It doesn't matter if it's two or three. Sound the alarm regardless of who responds. You are an awakened one. You sense the urgency of the hour. Don't look at the number of participants. The key is wholeheartedness and faith that prayer turns things around for God's glory. There has never been a single outpouring of the Spirit in the New Testament or in church history without a trumpeter seeing red skies and calling the assembly of saints to wholehearted prayer. Prophesying alone will not do it. Preaching alone will not do it. Social justice alone will not do it. Outpouring starts in the Upper Room chamber of encounter and is then released through acts of justice, preaching, and prophesying. But first, you must sound the alarm; call the saints to the altar of God and to wholeheartedness.

## RECEIVE THE CHARGE

### *Sound The Alarm: Five Keys to Wholehearted Wonder in Joel's Solemn Assembly*

The Apostle Peter connected the Upper Room encounter to Joel's prophecy about the outpouring of the Holy Spirit. One reason he could say this with confidence is because he knew that prior to this outpouring, the Upper Room saints were doing exactly what Joel said would happen before the outpouring. They were continuing steadfastly in prayer to God. Peter connected the Upper Room solemn assembly to Joel's solemn assembly.

There are at least five keys in Joel's solemn assembly that we can call our communities to engage in that will position us for a wholehearted response to God. Can you apply the five keys in Joel's Solemn Assembly to whole-hearted wonder over the next month? If so, please respond to each challenge below.

*Turn to Me with all your heart (wholehearted response)* (Joel 2:12).

1.  **Come lie all night in sackcloth** (Joel 1:13) – be willing to adjust your schedule for this. Have a start time but forget about the time it will end. Have a "persevere until" on your schedule. Having scheduled and timed prayer meeting is great, but every now then its wise to have a "go till the glory comes" prayer meeting. *Put on sackcloth -* Sackcloth was a garment made of coarse material that was really uncomfortable. We must embrace humility and get out of our comfort zones

2.  **Consecrate a fast** (Joel 1:14) – set apart a specific time for fasting together. Nothing tenderizes the heart quicker than fasting unto the Lord with determined prayer. It's just easier to say no to the flesh when it's weakened with fasting. It's easier

to give a wholehearted yes when our spirit is in charge.

3. **Call a sacred assembly** (Joel 1:14) – Private devotion is vital, as we mentioned in the previous chapter, but it is not enough to answer a national crisis. God requires corporate gatherings for prayer. *Sacred* "dedicated" or "set apart" to God. *The sacred assembly* speaks of its importance to God. Because God calls it sacred, it is to be important to us. What is of high priority to God must not be casual or optional to us. When the assembly is sacred, there are very few excuses for neglecting it.   Individual intercessors could not stop the coming judgment. We must gather. *"Even if these three men, Noah, Daniel, and Job, were in it, they would deliver only themselves by their righteousness," says the Lord GOD (Ezek. 14:14).*

4. **Gather elders** (leaders) and all inhabitants (families, children, etc.) (Joel 1:14).

5. **Cry out** (Joel 1:14) as with urgent and persistent prayer.

"…*it was a part of my creed to love everybody, but to fear no one; and I did not permit myself to believe any man could whip me till it was tried.*"

PETER CARTWRIGHT

# 13.

# THE UPPER
# ROOM GATE

## FIVE PREMISES TO ESTABLISH
## A CULTURE OF WONDER

---

PETER CARTWRIGHT IS A FAVORITE of mine. He was a Methodist preacher who had the nickname Old Rough and Ready. He was uncompromising in every sense of that word. One Sunday morning when he was about to preach, he was told that President Andrew Jackson was in the congregation. Cartwright was warned not to say anything out of line that might upset the President. So,

Cartwright walked up to the pulpit and began his message; "I understand that Andrew Jackson is here. I have been requested to be guarded in my remarks. Andrew Jackson will go to hell if he doesn't repent." The congregation was shocked and wondered how the president would respond. After the service, President Jackson shook hands with Peter Cartwright and said, "Sir, if I had a regiment of men like you, I could whip the world."[1]

Do you know what is even cooler than that? Peter Cartwright got saved in the wake of the Cane Ridge awakening. The good ground of Cane Ridge was a rich seedbed for planting the word of God in hearts, and the enemy couldn't steal it away. It was much like the old Pentecostals would say, "When you are born in the fire you won't settle for no smoke." That is what happens when you get saved in an awakening, you stay saved, and you impact others for Jesus. Cartwright was converted in revival fire, and the result was fiery preaching and, even more important, a fiery heart for Jesus. When we have an awareness of God's presence like they had at Cane Ridge, we are more likely to have disciples like Cartwright, utterly convinced of Heaven's priorities, fearless, and uncompromising.

Peter Cartwright surrendered his life to Jesus in the atmosphere of awe-filled awakening. Specifically, he was converted as a result of a devout prayer culture, with a real awareness of God's presence, marked by wonder, with preaching of the gospel that stuck to you. Is it no surprise that Cartwright could boldly proclaim the gospel to the President? He was born in wonder. Being born again in the atmosphere of God's presence, born in awakening, is the best seedbed for new disciples. If we desire to have fruit that remains, new converts must enter the environment of Spirit-led discipleship.

My Grandpa was a Freewill Baptist pastor who loved to see people born again and baptized. Like many pastors in rural America, he was bi-vocational, working at Ashland Oil and pastoring two small churches. He used to baptize people as soon as they would get saved. In the deep woods of West Virginia, they didn't baptize people in some fancy baptismal. No sir, you were baptized in those muddy creeks with the whole church standing on the creek bank watching, praying, and singing. One creek that got used for baptisms was called Twelve Pole. I know, that sounds real rural. You probably won't believe this, but I can even remember Grandpa busting ice in winter so that people could get baptized in this creek.

There was one particular brother in Grandpa's church that I will never forget, Brother Adkins. I can't forget Brother Adkins, because he was always getting baptized, re-baptized, and baptized again in order to make sure that he was saved. Brother Adkins had a stuttering problem, so when he would tell his stories of getting baptized again and again you couldn't help but smile. Whenever someone would bring up the subject of baptism, Brother Adkins would interrupt, "Why, why, why... Boys, I... I... I've been baptized so... so... so many times that ever fish in Twelve Pole knows my name."

We all loved Brother Adkins very much, but being baptized over and over for salvation is no proof of having "fruit that remains." Brother Adkins made it to the cross on Golgotha's hill. He even made his way into that glorious watery grave to lay his old life to rest with Christ and to be raised again with Him. But unfortunately, Brother Adkins never made his way to the Upper Room to be immersed in the Holy Spirit and be marked by lightning.

I believe many in the church pause somewhere between Passover and Pentecost. John the Baptist said that Jesus was not only the Lamb who takes away sin, but He is also the One who baptizes in the Holy Ghost and fire. We've preached well the glorious cross of our Savior and His resurrection, but we have not talked as much about the Upper Room baptism with the Spirit and fire. Today, our altars are full of rededications, and I'm not knocking that because I've been there several times. But I long to see a power released in preaching that marks people with God's stamp of salvation, with evidence of repentance, and a burning heart for Jesus. We need "fruit that remains." We need to once again ascend those stairs to the Upper Room, be filled with the Spirit, and come out with power that transforms lives forever.

## ASCENDING THE STAIRS
## TO THE UPPER ROOM

Imagine what it would've been like to be one of those Book of Acts saints that were immersed in Upper Room glory. Imagine what it would be like if you were a new believer and were immediately immersed into a praying community like the Upper Room, with an unshakable faith that Jesus is real, He is alive, and that He just might show up at random. Imagine that you've heard the stories of 500 people you know encountering Jesus after His death at one time. Like those Upper Room saints, you would've just heard that your friends saw Him at a fish breakfast by the sea, in a garden outside of His tomb, and on a journey to Emmaus. Imagine that you just heard that others saw Him appear in a room with the doors locked. What would it be like to have such an expectation everyday to encounter the presence of Jesus?

What mindset did the disciples take with them into the Upper Room prayer meeting? I believe they were thinking that Jesus is alive and He has ascended to His place of authority; so they expected to encounter the wonders of God through the promise of the Holy Spirit, then take this powerful encounter everywhere. What if each of us had the opportunity to be surrounded by this culture of faith? From the moment we first believed, we could turn the world upside down for Jesus.

Prior to entering the Upper Room these followers of Jesus had a unique framework upon which they could build a memorial in prayer before God. These building blocks would position them to receive the resolve they would need to labor in prayer until redemption history had turned. There are at least five premises that the early disciples took with them into the Upper Room solemn assembly:

## RECEIVE THE CHARGE

Here is summary of the five premises that we need to have in our hearts and minds to build an Upper Room culture of prayer. These premises strengthen our resolve to stay in the place of prayer until breakthrough. I encourage prayer leaders to highlight these truths again and again before and during prayer:

1. **Jesus' Words and Works Now Continue Through Us:** We enter the Upper Room with a mission to continue Jesus' words and works.

2. **Jesus Is Alive And We Are Witnesses To His Resurrection:** We enter the Upper Room with an expectation to encounter Jesus.

3. **Jesus Baptizes With The Holy Spirit:** We enter the Upper Room anticipating the fullness of the Holy Spirit.

4.  **Jesus has Ascended to the Right Hand of Power:**
    We enter the Upper Room praying from a position
    of authority.

5.  **Jesus Is Coming Back:** We enter the Upper Room
    to receive power to gather the end-time harvest.

—

*As they ministered to the Lord and fasted, the Holy Spirit said, "Now separate to Me Barnabas and Saul for the work to which I have called them." Then, having fasted and prayed, and laid hands on them, they sent them away.*

(ACTS 13:1-3)

—

# 14.

# PRIESTING BEFORE THE LORD

## EXPRESSING OUR ROLE AS PRIESTS UNTO JESUS

——

ONE WAY THAT WE CAN RELEASE wonder from our hearts is through what we call "Priesting Before the Lord." I believe the first time I heard this phrase was in a prayer meeting with a hero of mine, Lou Engle. It is simply the act of ministering to Jesus, doing the work of worship and the work of prayer. I have gone to church gatherings many times and said, "that song really ministered to me," or "that message really ministered to me." At Antioch in Acts 13 however, I don't believe they gave much thought to how the meeting would minister to them.

The church at Antioch came to minister to Jesus. Of course there is an exchange in worship when we give God glory. He then inhabits our praise and we receive. They approached the meeting ready to minister to Jesus, to make sure He receives the worship that He is so worthy of. Regardless of our feelings or what we want to receive, people of faith worship in the truth of who Jesus is and who they are to Him. We gather to minister to the heart of Jesus because He's worthy.

The church at Antioch "ministered to the Lord," which means, "to officiate as a priest, to do the work of worship, to do the work of prayer." To *minister* to the Lord was to *priest* before the Lord. This significant role of ministering before the Lord was real to them. They actually believed that their worship moved the heart of Jesus. They approached the meeting ready to do the *work of worship* and to do the *work of prayer*. Is worship work? Is prayer work? Not entirely, but there is an element of energy that we must give to it. Think of it as an investment in the relationship. I usually ask, "If there isn't any element of work to prayer why aren't more people doing it?" Worship and prayer are an enjoyable exercise, full of glory, and there is an element of my time and energy that I must give to it. The point is this; At Antioch, worship and prayer was something that they gave energy and effort to. Worship and prayer was not merely a posture of receptivity. They engaged God in worship, prayer, and fasting at first, then afterward the posture of receptivity came when the Holy Spirit started speaking.

## QUIET PRIVATE - PUBLIC RIOT

There is a place for receptivity in corporate and private prayer. I love contemplative prayer, the silent prayer of the heart. I am an introvert, so I get energy by getting alone and being quiet. It comes easy for me. As I've said, one of the most powerful fasts that I've ever been on was a "word" fast, where I practiced silence for seven days, not saying anything except when spoken to. I quieted the inward chatter in order to hear from God. It was glorious, and we all need quiet time with God alone. This is no new revelation, before it was popularly called soaking, there was a vast river throughout church history of desert fathers, monks, mystics, and theologians practicing silence and solitude. I can recommend no deeper way to open up your soul to God than getting alone with Him and entering into a baptism of silence with the intention of hearing His voice.

But when we gather as an Antioch, the posture isn't just receptivity; it's first ministry unto Jesus. Don't speak to me about an outpouring unless you're serious about doing Joel chapter one and two. There is no shred of biblical evidence or record in church history of a mighty outpouring of the Spirit through corporate-silent receptivity. There is no corporate soaking in Joel chapter one and two. There is only "priesting" before the Lord, crying loud, weeping between porch and altar, then after we do that God promises outpouring.

Let us daily get in that quiet place practicing solitude and silence alone with God. Let's cultivate that baptism of silence, hear His voice there, and then come to the gathering ready to minister to Jesus and release highest praises. I believe that if we each come to the prayer meeting, worship gathering, Sunday morning service ready to minister to Jesus, we will see the demonstration of the Kingdom.

Heaven comes to earth in many ways. The process of exchange from Heaven's dimension to ours is the process of sacrifice. As priests, a sure-fire sacrifice we now make is the sacrifice of praise. Through the new and living way, Jesus' blood, we have access to the holiest place in existence, and thereby bring the heavenly into our domain through our praises.

## NO SILENT SACRIFICE

*Therefore by Him let us continually offer the sacrifice of praise to God, that is, the fruit of our lips, giving thanks to His name* (Hebrews 13:15).

*"Therefore by Him..."* So many saints struggle with entering

into worship because they feel unworthy, guilty over sin, or they feel like God is mad at them. The only way to "enter in" is through the blood of Jesus. There must be a mind renewal take place. When we approach corporate gatherings we must think upon His righteousness and His free gift of salvation to those who believe. If you are in covenant with God through Jesus, the wrath of God that was against you has now been appeased. God's not mad at believers in Jesus. His blood has appeased God's wrath. Does the Father discipline those He loves? Of course, God refuses to leave us hindered by sin, broken, and unloved. His discipline is to help us experience deeper measures of His love. Is God's wrath upon those who are outside of covenant with Jesus? Of course, but that's not you. Because of our faith in Jesus, we have free access to God's throne.

Now that it's real to us that Jesus' blood has given us access to Heaven's dimensions, the only proper response is an open mouth overflowing with thanksgiving. If you really get what Jesus had done for you, you'll give a worthy offering of praise. I can't imagine anyone truly receiving the unthinkable forgiveness of God through Jesus and not wanting to go wholehearted in praise. When you receive an unthinkable gift, a surprise that blows your mind, you know you don't deserve, in front of the whole world, the last thing you could imagine yourself doing is giving some passive response of more receptivity. Now, there's a time for the receptive posture, but when the forgiven gather it's time to celebrate. I can't say for others, but I'm still tripping over the fact that He loves me. The King must be crazy for loving me. His love is like lightning, shocking my heart with His majesty. I've got to respond to that love with high praise.

When we come to God through the merits of Jesus alone, we cannot just *think* a praise, we've got to *say* a praise. The writer of Hebrews spells out for us exactly what he means by a sacrifice of praise, "the fruit of our lips giving thanks to His name." Clapping alone won't do it. The worship leader up front singing won't do it. I must open my mouth, regardless of how I feel, and begin to minister to Jesus with my praise. Why? He's worthy. When the Holy Spirit bears witness with your spirit that you are a child of God, you want to say with all you have how much you love Jesus for taking away the rejection, the shame, and the guilt. The Holy Spirit makes our sonship real to us. Saints, we've been adopted. We've been redeemed. What slave scarred by sins shackles can hold their tongue when finally free? In this context, silence is irreverent and dishonoring. When love melts your hang-ups you'll ask yourself "what have I been doing holding my praise inside?" When you really get it that Jesus loves you recklessly, without concern of what you've done, you'll find your identity as a priest to be the greatest privilege you have, to offer Him the fruit of your lips giving thanks to His name.

## CROWNED PRIESTHOOD

*But you are a chosen generation, a royal priesthood,*
*a holy nation, His own special people, that you may*
*proclaim the praises of Him who called you out of*
*darkness into His marvelous light* (I Peter 2:9).

When the weight of what's happened for us through Jesus' blood begins to evoke awe-filled wonder in our hearts, we begin to experience a crowning of our identity as priests. Every New Testament believer is a *"Royal* Priest" (I Peter 2:9). Think of the implications of that for a moment. We are "A royal (kingly-governing-ruling) priesthood." A royal priesthood, under the headship of Jesus is one of honor, dignity, and privilege. With royal authority, these priests minister to Jesus. This priesthood has been crowned and exalted to the same rank as a king, with no darkness having dominion over them and nothing earthly controlling them but God through Jesus. In Jesus, we've received the crowning of Priesthood and are consecrated to God for offering spiritual sacrifices and releasing His purposes through our worship and intercession. This is so important, because it tells us about our identity, to be priests who are crowned with authority to govern with our prayers and worship to Jesus.

Notice, we are not a "Priestly Royal," but we are a "Royal Priesthood." A "Priestly Royal" would be a king or royal figure who does "priestly" things through "royal" methods. A "Royal Priesthood" is one who is a priest doing royal things through "priestly" methods. If you take a King and ask him to do "priestly" things, he will do so in a "kingly" way, because that is who he is. He's a king, which is his identity. If you take a Priest and ask him to do "kingly" things, he will do so in a "priestly" way, because that is who is. *By crowning the priesthood, Jesus is installing Priests to do "Kingly" things through "Priestly" methods.* We have been crowned as priests in order to show forth His praises. In other words, you are going to go to war, just as a king would, but because you are a priest, you'll aim at devotion to Yahweh and He'll war on your behalf as give yourself to Him in intercession, filling incense bowls, playing harps, and giving a sacrifice of praise.

There are many today trying to do priestly things with kingly methods, trying to carry the ark with Philistine methods. Kingly thinking just wants to get the ark into town no matter how it's done. The king, in this context, is much more pragmatic than priestly. The priest is primarily concerned with how our decisions will express worship. The priest makes decisions knowing that our worship and prayer will determine how we rule as kings.

The church at Antioch approached gatherings ready to minister to Jesus, because they understood their identity as priests. Our prayer and worship meetings are healthy when they understand Jesus' role as our great High Priest, and through His blood He has made us Priests. Your focus will be to minister to Jesus. I can just hear the church at Antioch saying, "What ever we do in this meeting, lets make sure we minister to Jesus. Let our worship, our prayers, and prophecies bring pleasure to His heart. He is on the throne and He is so worthy of our worship."

The church at Antioch served as a catalyst for Christian witness. They had heartfelt devotion to Jesus through worship and fasting. They took seriously their need for prophetic ministry and hearing from God for direction. They sent missionaries embracing Acts 1:8, to be witnesses unto Jesus in all the earth. Where the Jerusalem harvest in Acts 2 depended on the masses coming to Jerusalem, Antioch would be a springboard for missionaries to be sent out to reap the harvest. All of these efforts flowed from Antioch's primary focus to "Priest" before the Lord. The result: missionary zeal. Our mission, our assignment, and our dream all flow from learning to Priest before the Lord in prayer and praise. Antioch was a church where worship, prayer, fasting, prophetic ministry, and sending missionaries converged, but the primary focus was the presence of Jesus. As they "ministered to the Lord," they received God's dream for Barnabas and Saul.

The impact for the Kingdom of God that came out of this dynamic Church is immeasurable, because this is where Paul received His commission. This marks Paul's first missionary journey. If it had not been for this praying, fasting, prophesying, and missionary-sending community, we probably wouldn't have the Apostle Paul's impact. Antioch was so dear to Paul that nearly each transition in His missions work would begin at Antioch. The Lord wants to converge all of the dynamics of ministry found at Antioch for the End-time Harvest to release more divinely sent missionaries as He did with Paul and Barnabas.

## RECEIVE THE CHARGE

### *Practical Approaches to "Priesting" before the Lord*

1. **Rally Around Jesus:** Focus on Jesus – to minister to the Lord. Regardless of how we feel, we worship in truth. We celebrate who Jesus and who we are to Him, a crowned priesthood.

2. **Embrace Your Privileges as a Royal Priest:** Accept Jesus' free gift of right standing with God, approach the throne through the blood of Jesus, and open your forgiven heart with praises on you're your lips. Proclaim the praises. Enter His gates with thanksgiving and His courts with praise. Proclaim the glory of God, and keep up the remembrance of His wondrous deeds in the earth.

3. **Learn to Linger:** Don't be in hurry to leave the

presence of God.  Learn to hang out, linger in the presence of God.  Pray in the Spirit for long periods of time.  Repeat short phrases to God that glorify His majesty (You are holy.  You are worthy.  There is none like you).

4.  **Practice a Fasted Lifestyle:**  The church at Antioch ministered to the Lord through their prayers and fasting.  Fasting can be an expression of our worship to God.  Fasting empties us and moves the heart towards God and others.  Antioch became sensitive to the Holy Spirit's leadership as they fasted.

5.  **Release Prophetic Activity:**  Antioch positioned themselves to hear God speak as they ministered to the Lord through prayer and fasting.  "The Holy Spirit said…"  As we "priest" before the Lord expect to hear from God.  Release that sound you hear as He leads.

*The grace of the Lord Jesus Christ, and the love of God, and the communion of the Holy Spirit be with you all.*

(2 CORINTHIANS 13:14)

*The Holy Spirit… will teach you all things.*

(JOHN 14:26)

*The Spirit of truth…will guide you into all truth; He will tell you things to come.*

(JOHN 16:13)

*The anointing…abides in you, and you do not need that anyone teach you; but as the same anointing teaches you concerning all things.*

(1 JOHN 2:27)

# 15.

# WIND ALWAYS
# TO YOUR BACK

———

Taking the sense of wonder public requires us to be carried along by the Holy Spirit. The benediction of Saint Patrick has a line in it that reads, "May the wind be always at your back." It's a picture of a person being borne along by the wind of God, the Holy Spirit. Rather than opposing the direction the Spirit is leading, the call is to have the wind carrying us into the plans of the Father. Being able to say, "I come with the wind at my back" means that I come with the empowering feeling of being sent. Heaven is backing me up on this one.

According to the prophecy given by Jesus, the Holy Spirit would empower the Upper Room disciples to be His adventurous witnesses in Jerusalem, Judea, Samaria, and the utter most parts of the earth with the wind at their back. To do this, they were going to need a guide. The Holy Spirit was going to make them a prophetic people, a people that could be led by the Spirit and fulfill the mission of Jesus. The Book of Acts Church was immersed in prophetic activity. They took seriously the mission of God, and therefore needed to be sensitive to the leading of the Holy Spirit for effective witness. They valued God's leadership, so they needed to value His voice. They were a prophetic people having the ability to hear clearly and release what was on God's heart. The disciples' ability to hear and obey the leadership of the Spirit turned mission into adventure.

> *And it shall come to pass in the last days, says God, That I will pour out of My Spirit on all flesh; Your sons and your daughters shall prophesy, Your young men shall see visions, Your old men shall dream dreams. And on My menservants and on My maidservants I will pour out My Spirit in those days; And they shall prophesy* (Acts 2:17-18).

## WHAT THE HOLY SPIRIT
## LIKES TO TALK ABOUT

As God, the Holy Spirit can speak however He chooses. He is the inspiration behind every author of the Old and New Testament, so we have plenty of content to see what He likes to talk about and what is important to Him (2 Sam. 23:2; Isaiah 59:21; Jer. 1:9; 2 Tim. 3:15-17; 2 Pet. 1:21; John 14:25, 26; 1 Cor. 2:13; 1 Thess. 4:15; Rev. 1:10, 11; 2:7). Speaking in the most general of terms, we can gain tremendous revelation into what kind of things the Holy Spirit likes to talk about just by reading the bible. That is usually where I start with someone who asks, "How do I know that the Holy Spirit is speaking to me." Of course, we start by asking, "Does it agree with what He has already said in the bible?"

**When the Holy Spirit speaks we can be confident that:**
1. He brings honor to the person of Jesus Christ.
2. He produces a greater hatred of sin and a greater love for holiness.
3. He produces a greater respect and love for the content of the bible.
4. He leads people into truth.
5. He produces a greater love for God and man.

We need to ask ourselves, "Does what I hear bring

honor to the person of Jesus Christ? Does it stir me to get rid of sin and provoke me to love and good works?" This is speaking in general terms of what kind of things the Holy Spirit will say.

Beyond the general, we can also know exactly what the Holy Spirit talks about by looking at what He says to specific individuals in the book of Acts. The Holy Spirit is pointed in His choice of words in Acts. We have specific verses that say, "The Holy Spirit said…" Keep in mind that the Holy Spirit inspired Luke to record the Book of Acts, so He is the one prompting Luke to record the things He says. It's as if the Holy Spirit is saying, "Luke, here is what I want you to say that I said."

There are three versus in Acts where it clearly gives us specific things that God the Holy Spirit says, and I believe they are precious to Him. They give us revelation into the mind of the Holy Spirit and into things He likes to talk about, the things He wants to be remembered for saying throughout history, throughout eternity. It gets me every time I say it: "The Holy Spirit inspired Luke to write, 'The Holy Spirit said…'"

### GO AND JOIN:
#### *The Spirit Imparts the Divine Go*

The first saying of the Holy Spirit in Acts is to Philip: "*Then* the Spirit said to Philip, "Go near and overtake (join) this chariot" (Acts 8:26-29). The Holy Spirit's message to Phillip was "Go join."

> Now an angel of the Lord spoke to Philip, saying, "Arise and go toward the south along the road which goes down from Jerusalem to Gaza." This is desert. So he arose and went. And behold, a man of Ethiopia, a eunuch of great authority under Candace the queen of the Ethiopians, who had charge of all her treasury, and had come to Jerusalem to worship, was returning. And sitting in his chariot, he was reading Isaiah the prophet. Then the Spirit said to Philip, "Go near and overtake this chariot (Acts 8:2629).

Philip was able to tell the treasurer of the kingdom of Ethiopia (a man of a different culture and ethnicity) the good news about Jesus, and the man was baptized a Christian. When the Holy Spirit speaks, He calls us to take action and meet people where they are (to go join ourselves to their chariot). The Spirit's message to Phillip was "Go." The Holy Spirit could've inspired Luke to write down any number of things that He said. However, the Holy Spirit chose to record forever, "I said to Phillip, Go and join..." This is what's on His heart; it's what He wants to talk about. Always obey every impulse of the Spirit to "Go and join" yourself to someone's chariot, to some conversation, to a person in need of hearing the good news of Jesus.

The Holy Spirit has nations in mind with His charge for Phillip to "Go." He is orchestrating the fulfillment of Jesus' prophecy in Acts 1:8, that the disciples of Jesus would be baptized in the Holy Spirit and receive power to be His witnesses in all the earth. They were receiving the divine "Go." The Holy Spirit loves to release wind in our sails to go. Have you ever had the Holy Spirit release a "Go and join" yourself to something? If so, you know what it feels like to gain energy from doing the Father's will. The momentum in your heart is life-giving. His "Go" will un-bog you when you're stuck in fear. Saints, I've got bible on it; the Holy Spirit likes to say, "Go and join."

## GO AND DOUBT NOTHING:
### *The Spirit Imparts Faith*

The second saying of the Holy Spirit in Acts is to Peter:

> "*While Peter thought about the vision, the Spirit said to him, "Behold, three men are seeking you. 20 Arise therefore, go down and go with them, doubting nothing; for I have sent them*" (Acts 10:19, 20).

From this passage, we begin to see a pattern. As He said

"Go" to Phillip, the Holy Spirit is once again giving someone direction by telling them to "Go," but this time to Peter. There is more. In this passage we also see that when the Holy Spirit speaks, He speaks faith. As our comforter and teacher, the Holy Spirit will call us into places that challenge our faith. He said, *"go with them doubting nothing"*. He will also speak things to us that encourage our faith as well. He also said, *"for I have sent them"*.

The Holy Spirit's message to Peter was "Doubt nothing." *Doubting*, in this context literally means, *to fight against yourself*. It is that sort of doubting that causes people to end up hesitating when they should be making moves. It is doubt that produces delayed obedience. The Holy Spirit will speak to us in ways that remove doubt. Apparently, faith is one of the things He really likes to talk about. If we will have ears to hear, the Holy Spirit will speak revelation over us that removes any misgivings, any division in our decision-making. When the Holy Spirit imparts faith by speaking to us, He removes the wavering between hope and fear. When the Holy Spirit speaks, He removes doubt and imparts faith.

## GO AND WORK:
### *The Spirit Builds Teams and Gives Assignments*

The third saying of The Holy Spirit in Acts was to Barnabas and Saul (Paul):

*"...the Holy Spirit said, Now Separate Barnabas and Saul to Me, for the work to which I have called them"* (Acts 13:2). *As they ministered to the Lord and fasted, the Holy Spirit said, "Now separate to Me Barnabas and Saul for the work to which I have called them." Then, having fasted and prayed, and laid hands on them, they sent them away"* (Acts 13:2, 3).

From this saying of the Holy Spirit, we can see that He speaks about your mission, your calling, and your assignment. I'd even say that He is still releasing a divine "Go" in this context as well. Specifically, what the Holy Spirit said to Barnabas and Saul was "work." The Holy Spirit speaks to us about our calling. There is hardly anything more encouraging than to know who you are to God and that He wants to partner with you to see His works accomplished. You have a mission; the Holy Spirit will speak to you about it again and again.

## When the Holy Spirit speaks in the Book of Acts

1. **He Speaks about PEOPLE:** He's focused on leading us into our individual callings that result in reaching others and expanding the Kingdom of Jesus. He's interested in speaking to our callings in order to bring forth God's redemptive purposes.

2. **He Speaks about our MISSION**:  He focuses on establishing the Government of Jesus in human hearts and lives.  He apparently likes the words "Go" and "Work."

3. **He Speaks FAITH**:  Each of these statements we looked at undoubtedly challenged the hearers to a greater place of trust in God, but they also produced unwavering confidence and trust in God's calling for them in that moment, because they all did as they were directed.

---

### RECEIVE THE CHARGE

*Positioning Ourselves to Hear
the Holy Spirit Speak*

There are at least five contexts where the Holy Spirit speaks in the Book of Acts.  You can position yourself as the book of Acts saints did to hear His voice.  Do you need to hear from God?  Expect to hear the Holy Spirit's voice.  Actively listen in these contexts:

1. **In Private Prayer** – Peter was in private prayer on the rooftop when he received the vision.

2. **In Corporate Prayer** – Barnabas and Saul were at a

corporate gathering when they received their call to work.

3.  **In Fasting –** The Church gathered at Antioch ministered to the Lord in fasting and prayer when they heard the voice of the Spirit.

4.  **In Meditation of Scripture** (or in Peter's case, a vision) "as Peter thought about the vision, the Holy Spirit said..."

5.  **In Mission:** On the Go, In the Assignment, About Others (Phillip was on the Go). The Holy Spirit speaks to those who are already moving.

# 16.

# LOST IN WONDER
# AND GUIDED BY GLORY

## RELEASING WONDER
## IN UNCHARTED WATERS

———

THERE IS A SAYING OF THE HOLY SPIRIT in Acts that most people miss. It could be argued that He says this to us more than He says anything else. This message of the Holy Spirit in the book of Acts is to Paul and Silas (on Paul's 2nd Missionary Journey): *"...they were forbidden by the Holy Spirit to preach the word in Asia"* (Acts 16:6). The Holy Spirit's message to Paul and Silas was "No."

> *Now when they had gone through Phrygia and the region of Galatia, they were forbidden by the Holy Spirit to preach the word in Asia. After they had come to*

*Mysia, they tried to go into Bithynia, but the Spirit did not permit them. So passing by Mysia, they came down to Troas. And a vision appeared to Paul in the night. A man of Macedonia stood and pleaded with him, saying, 'Come over to Macedonia and help us.' Now after he had seen the vision, immediately we sought to go to Macedonia, concluding that the Lord had called us to preach the gospel to them* (Acts 16:610).

The text doesn't say how the Spirit communicated this "No." It may have been through inner promptings, prophetic utterance, or external circumstances. We don't know. What we do know is that the Holy Spirit changed their plans twice (vs. 6 *"forbidden to preach in Asia"* and vs. 7 *"they tried to make their way to Bythynia and could not"*). They didn't get a "Yes" until they made it to Troas (771 land miles from where they began in Lystra). In my mind, it is always a good idea to plan a mission anytime, anywhere. In this case, the Holy Spirit forbids this apostolic team from preaching in the places they had planned. Apparently, Paul made plans in pencil, stayed flexible, mobile, and adaptable. If we are going to be people of the Kingdom, we don't have time for good ideas, only God-ideas. We've got to plan and strategize but leave room for the Holy Spirit to call "audible's", and adjust our sails to His wind.

Paul continues being faithful with what revelation he's

been given, going forward until he get's a *Yes*. I can imagine the team asking him, "Where to, Paul?" Paul says, "I don't know, keep marching." What dependency is required when God guides with a *No*?

## SOMETIMES GOD'S "YES" COMES AFTER SEVERAL "NO'S"

How we handle God's *No* reveals our commitment to the mission of Jesus. The Apostle Paul simply obeyed even though he genuinely had a great plan in place. He trusted God's answer, knowing that His plan is always the priority. God answers prayer in many different ways, and all of them are trustworthy. When God answers prayer, He may say:

- "Yes, I thought you'd never ask? Here you go."
- "Yes, and I'll go above and beyond what you're asking."
- "Yes, but you don't have a clue what you're asking for."
- "Yes, but not yet."
- "No, I've got something better."
- "No, because I love you."

To be clear, God doesn't say *No* to His promises. His promises are *Yes and Amen*. But we do see in the Word where guidance, direction, and even discipline can come from God saying, *No.* We must not squirm and fight the Father's loving *No.* For Paul and Silas, the Holy Spirit really said *No* and *Yes.* He said *No* to a specific idea but *Yes* to the overall mission and vision. Paul and Silas obeyed and just kept moving until they had further clarity. The result was many lives getting changed in Macedonia, including the cities of Philippi and Thessalonica.

When God said *No,* Paul still maintained a sense of adventure and moved forward. He kept his wow factor. I imagine Paul smiling as he traveled those roads discerning the Spirit's direction. It doesn't matter where the road takes him, because he found a glory on the roads of this life. He was on the road called Damascus when he encountered the glory of Jesus. Paul was still lost in the wonder of that encounter on the road to Damascus and was guided by that glory since. He recounts that marking moment again and again. I can almost hear him saying, *"Jesus has been changing my direction, my plans, my good ideas since the Damascus road. I've been lost in wonder and guided by glory. I'm just excited about the adventure in Jesus. It's my joy. I'm still on these roads and I'm still following His lead everyday."* I think Paul had the same mind that Moses had when he told God that he wasn't going to move forward unless God's presence was guiding him there (Exodus 33).

## LINKING UP FOR LEGACY

The two most important connections requiring the Holy Spirit's leadership in terms of assignment and mission are people and places. An assignment can rise or fall based on the people you run with and where you run together. Because Paul was sensitive to the leadership of the Holy Spirit he was divinely connected to the right people and places. If we are not sensitive to the Holy Spirit's leadership in these areas we can give our loyalties to people and places without leaving a legacy. By loyalties I mean allegiances and firm support. I can only give that to Jesus and the people He's calling me to yoke arms with. By legacy I mean something that will continue on beyond my involvement. Legacy in the Kingdom of Jesus is about establishing something for others to climb upon and go higher than we have. This will never happen without the leadership of the Spirit connecting us to our assigned places and people.

*Linking up with the right people.* In Acts 16, Paul and Silas connect with Timothy. These three are *"forbidden to preach in Asia"* and *"they tried to make their way to Bythynia and could not."* God told them "no." They faithfully obeyed God's leadership. All the while God had an apostolic connection awaiting them that eventually left a legacy, touching every generation, that will forever be celebrated in heaven. The Apostle Luke was waiting for them in Troas and was about to join their team. As he writes the book of Acts, he inserts himself into the narrative as an eyewitness to Paul's missionary journeys by saying, "…sailing from Troas, we…" Up to this point in Acts, Luke describes Paul's journeys by saying "they." They left a legacy that touched earth and will be remembered in heaven. Thanks to this connection with Luke, these missionary journeys made it into the inspired Word of God, the book of Acts, to be shared with billions of lives and every generation into the age eternal.

God may change our plans again and again, but if we trust Him and continue to follow His leading He will connect us with people that will multiply our efforts to expand the Kingdom of Jesus. This is what it means to be guided by glory and lost in wonder. If you'll commit to follow His presence and His leading, you'll end up with impact that can only be measured in eternity. If you've been told *No* by the Lord, trust Him, He may have a "Luke" on the other side of your act of obedience that will enable you to leave a Kingdom legacy.

*Linking up with the right place.* It is interesting to note that Paul was thinking of doing land missions, but God had a sea voyage planned into what was uncharted waters for the Kingdom of God. You need to be thinking, *"what's on the other side of this act of obedience?"* For Paul, his faithfulness with God's *No* would eventually pay off, as he would later receive clarity in the Macedonian call while in Troas. Paul committed to be guided by a glorious vision. A vision appeared to Paul in the night, a man of Macedonia stood and pleaded with him, saying, "Come over to Macedonia and help us."

Paul received this vision in Alexandria Troas, a port city. All along this journey, Paul had been thinking land missions, while God was thinking uncharted waters and new territories. Paul ended up writing three New Testament letters to this region, one to Philippi and two letters for Thessalonica. You may have a different plan altogether, but you must trust that God's ways are higher, better, and will ultimately bring greater glory to Jesus than our best strategies and ideas. We must commit to the process of hearing and obeying regardless of our how fruitless it may at first appear.

When the glory is your guide, you'll avoid disappointment and walk in the appointment God has for you. You may be in a situation where you do not have all the details, maybe with closed doors on every side. Commit to the prophetic process. Wait until there is clarity from heaven. Look for those opportunities where there is a desperate man urgently calling for help. You have an appointment at Troas! Just jumping into things without God's leading usually ends up in disappointment. Disappointment will lull the wow-factor. We avoid this by being led by the Holy Spirit into all truth. What's the vision God has given you? What's in there? Don't let anything quench that flame. What do you have faith for? Space is not the final frontier; the Kingdom Dimension is! Maybe all these doors have been closing because God has something in store that you haven't even considered yet. Like Paul, you may be in for uncharted waters. Cultivate a sense of adventure as you're lead by the Spirit. The dimension of God's Kingdom is the final frontier of exploration. It is vast, it is huge, it is overwhelmingly wonderful, and Jesus wants us to search it out first.

## RECEIVE THE CHARGE

1. Have you ever had a No from the Lord? How did you respond? If so, how have you maintained a sense of adventure and moved forward?

2. In times of transition, how have you been sensitive to the Holy Spirit's voice? Did God connect you with the right people and right places?

*Let them praise His name with the dance... Let the high praises of God be in their mouth, and a two-edged sword in their hand, To execute vengeance on the nations, and punishments on the peoples; To bind their kings with chains, and their nobles with fetters of iron; To execute on them the written judgment— This honor have all His saints. Praise the Lord.*

(PSALMS 149:3, 6-9)

# 17.

# RELEASE THE SOUND

UNLOCKING TOMORROWS
OUTPOURING TODAY

———

THE CITY OF MEMPHIS HAS A tremendously moving musical history. The impact it has had on shaping American popular music cannot be overstated. The Sun recordings of Elvis Presley in the fifties alone could establish Memphis as a catalyst city for music, but Memphis is known for so many other voices that impacted the culture: Johnny Cash, Carl Perkins, Roy Orbison, Howlin' Wolf, Booker T. and M.G.s, Otis Redding, Rufus and Carla Thomas, Isaac Hayes, Albert King, Sam and Dave, and "The Reverend" Al Green, just to list a few.

Memphis was the potter's wheel for shaping all

subsequent rock and roll, blues, gospel, sixties soul music, seventies funk music, rhythm and blues, rockabilly, and country. The synthesis of black and white music that occurred in the 1950's in Memphis was unique. In a city overrun with racial tension, black and white musicians came together and produced a whole new sound that resulted in decades of musical impact and birthed something brand new. They called it the "Memphis Sound."

Before the civil rights movement of the sixties there was a sound being released by a few blacks and whites united in song ten years earlier, in the fifties. Before there was any evidence of blacks and whites being united on anything, there was sound embodying a future reality. With segregation still looming and racism at its peak, these black and white musicians came together as forerunners of a future freedom and released the sound of a few that eventually became a sight in the entire nation. With no evidence of breakthrough for justice in the land, they sang anyway and became a demonstration of what was coming.

I believe the musical impact of Memphis is a beautiful picture that can bring encouragement for today's voices that are declaring tomorrow's outpouring. Faith comes by hearing a sound. Awakening is a sound before it is a sight. Freedom is declared before it is delivered. Reformation is a voice before it is a vehicle of change. *We see something in the Spirit that is coming, and with little or no evidence of it in the land we release the sound of it.* We understand that God will release the breakthrough when He will, but we are going to do everything we can to get into position to receive what it will look like, then do our best by grace to announce it's coming.

I do not mean that we are just describing a future outpouring. That will never do. We are shaping the future with the words we release in agreement with Jesus. We must abandon our doctrines of procrastination and push the issue of revival in the Church and awakening in the culture by setting apart our voices for a holy purpose. We are prophetically leaning into tomorrow's breakthrough, not merely describing what is coming; we are creating it with our prayers and prophecies.

## PREACH FAITH UNTIL YOU HAVE IT

Peter Böhler was a young Moravian that had a profound impact on John Wesley during a time of spiritual crisis. Wesley had been searching for answers to the longings of his heart. He felt as though he lacked the faith required for salvation even though he was preaching the gospel daily. Wesley told Peter Böhler that he was going to stop preaching, for how could he preach to others a faith that he, himself, lacked? Böhler counseled Wesley: "Preach faith *till* you have it, and then, because you have it, you *will* preach faith." The truth is still the truth, whether we believe it or not. If we find it in the bible we can proclaim it with confidence, even if it hasn't reached our experience fully yet.

Can a teacher of the bible teach on the subject of marriage if the teacher has never been married? The answer is yes, if they teach from the bible. Can a sick man say that God heals? Of course he can, because we have evidence in the bible that God heals. We preach faith until we have it. We preach miracles until we have them. We give the call to establish dwelling places for God even before there is any evidence on the land of God having a resting place.

The Word of God is truth regardless. This bible is the foundation from which we pray, proclaim, and sing, about the coming of Jesus. We do this because we see this truth in the bible. When it comes to awakening and cultural transformation, we search the biblical record for what God says about it, and we release the sound of what's coming by faith and not by sight.

## SANCTIFYING THE SOUND

There is a faith principle in the book of Joshua that many miss. I'm guilty of it. We focus on the moment of victory, the crazy-loud shout that brought the walls of Jericho down, but we miss the prep-time that Joshua invested in the men of war and the people under his leadership before the walls fell flat at their shout. Yes, Joshua 6:20 is a faith-charged story that reveals what God did in a moment with the people's shout, but Joshua 6:10 is what positioned them to release a sound so set-apart to God that no barrier of the enemy could withstand it.

Before there was a shout that brought the walls down, Joshua commanded the people, "…You shall NOT SHOUT or make ANY NOISE with your VOICE, nor shall A WORD proceed out of your MOUTH, until the day I say to you SHOUT!" (6:10). It was a short, loud, power-packed shout that brought down Jericho's walls, but it was six days of total silence that positioned the people to release such a faith-filled sound (Joshua 6:3; 14).

The people took a deep breath before they released the winds of God's justice from their lungs and over their vocal cords. Their shout had something on it. Their sound was about to inaugurate the possession of their promise. This sound came from the overflow of a set-apart heart and from a deep breath of silence. Can you imagine spending an entire day without one word coming out of your mouth? What about six days? Joshua's charge to keep silence set a guard over their mouths and prevented them from speaking unbelief.

Here is the faith principle we miss in Joshua 6; we must

set apart our voices for God's purpose when marching around our Jericho. Having set apart our voices we can release the sound that unlocks our future inheritance. Joshua's wise leadership to call the people to total silence for six days surely indicates that he had in mind the forty years of wilderness wondering and the people's inability to possess God's promises because they kept complaining. Their complaining was evidence of their unbelief. Their unbelief kept them from entering into their inheritance. Silence was the cure.

In addition, Joshua was mindful of the negative report of the spies that disheartened the people. Now, facing Jericho, Joshua called them to silence and he forbids any words of doubt and unbelief from escaping their lips. We cannot have a victim mentality and possess a victor's inheritance. We can't survey the moral landscape in our nations and become immobilized at how bad it is. We must be careful that we are not adopting a worldview that believes darkness is advancing and we are fighting a loosing battle. Laying down your victor's crown for a victim mentality will bury you without ever entering into the promise land.

This charge to keep silence before God enabled them to make their words holy and to no longer sin with their speech. When facing challenges or delays, refuse to glance at the strength of Jericho's walls and instead look to the Lord Jesus, the Author and Finisher of your faith. Don't look at the size of your army compared to the masses against you. Only give voice to what you believe in agreement with God's promise.

Abiding in the vine isn't only about speaking words of faith in agreement with Jesus. It is also a refusal to speak words that are contrary to Christ's words and His promises ("If you remain in Me and My WORDS remain in you..." Jn. 15:7). Forbid your tongue to speak contrary to what you have spoken in faith towards God. Your words in agreement with Jesus' words have power. Right now you have the power to impart the grace of God to others with your words. Use your mouth to be someone's necessary edification today. You can actually move someone into position to receive God's empowering grace with your faith-filled words. Speak the word only, silence unbelief, and you will position yourself to release a faith-filled shout that brings down God's enemies.

Having set apart our speech through silence, we are now positioned to release a sound that charges the atmosphere with faith. We can unlock tomorrow's outpouring today. *It is a principle of the kingdom: The demonstration of the Spirit follows a declaration of a believer.* The Spirit moves as the Word is spoken. We must release the sound of what's coming into the earth from heaven, and we'll begin to see the Spirit move on the Word.

There are several great resources available today on the power of our faith's confession, the authority of the believer, and the principles of intercession. I love to study those subjects. However, I wanted to go a bit deep into those here. I may have fallen short of my goal but what I hoped to do here is to encourage you to release what God has been revealing to you that's just over the horizon. Paint a picture for your generation of a world that honors Jesus. Like those Memphis musicians, you're releasing a sound of a coming freedom even though there is real bondage and pain in your region still all around you. I can just imagine those musicians, just a few of them, not doing what everyone else in the culture was doing, coming together and with guitars and keyboards they sang in a revolution. They released a sound.

## RECEIVE THE CHARGE

Spend a week in silence. If you have responsibilities at work or at home that will not allow total silence, simply become more aware of the inner chatter of your heart. Become aware of what immediately comes out of your mouth when pressured. Sometimes you can practice silence by speaking only when spoken to. Keep a smile on your face. Don't be rude to people. If you have to talk, do it. Then when the opportunity arises, enter back into silence. The goal is to sanctify our speech for a holy purpose. The goal is to hear from the Lord. The goal is to remove unbelief from our lips. Record your discoveries in a journal.

———

*"The fire on the altar
is to be kept burning
continually, it is not
to go out."*

(LEVITICUS 6:13)

———

# 18.

# SUSTAINING WONDER

———

THE MOST COMMON QUESTION I get from students and friends is, "How do I keep the fire burning?" I recommend that you start making lightning; position yourself before the throne of God to encounter His majestic glory. I recommend the way of wonder. It is a means to walk, everyday, in the fire of first love. The way of wonder energizes your heart to connect with God. Wonder is both an energizer toward God and the result of being close to God. Wonder is sparked in the heart as we encounter the lightning of God. His lightning, His majesty, and His glory melt our hearts. As we resolve to protect that tender place with God, we live fully alive. We live easily moved to whole-hearted love. A wonder-filled heart can even be moved toward God in the midst of life's worst storms. How do I sustain wonder?

A wonder-filled heart is sustained by consistent application of ordinary principles. Ninety percent of the battle to sustain wonder is simply showing up to the private prayer closet everyday. There is no special prayer anointing that someone has and others do not. You've got to show up. You've got to "come to be in the Spirit."

Wonder wanes when we disconnect in our conversations with God. I'm speaking of real conversation. Wonder is sustained as we talk with God as an involved Father. We ask God questions. We rehearse our love legacy, our memories with God. Wonder will not wane if we consistently apply ordinary principles, if we simply show up everyday with expectation.

It is not a big flame that God is after but a continual-daily one that doesn't go out. The continual flame is going to require effort but not nearly as much as trying to build a large one that God hasn't commanded. There is an element of energy that we must give to our devotional lives to keep the fire burning. But it's a consistent fuel that this continual flame needs, not just large sporadic dowses. It's what I do everyday consistently that will produce the flame God requires.

I find it fascinating that Jesus calls John the Baptist a "burning and shinning lamp." See that? He's burning. His flame is continual. He's "shinning;" he's a steady source of light. He's a "lamp" and not a massive engulfing flame. God is the only all-consuming fire! Jesus is the only "big deal." He gets all of the glory. God is after the constant, steady, living flame on the altar of your heart.

Many get this twisted and focus on a *big* sense of wonder rather than a *steady* sense of wonder. I don't have to tell you where the "Go Big or Go Home" approaches to ministry and church life have left many burning altars, burning preachers, and burning servants burned out. The mechanics may still be there but the fire is out. Jesus has come and removed their lamp stand and they continue on in blissful ignorance.

Many spend themselves attempting to build something impressive only to over-reach, over-extend, and over-do. Imagine the energy it would take for the priests to maintain a great big fire in the Temple. Surely, it would be up and down, bigger one moment than it is the next, and in constant flux. The priests would be surrounded by the drama of an up and down experience with God. When we focus on big impact alone we are trying to build something that is going to require too much human control to maintain it. It's over-reaching. The Bible calls over-reaching covetousness. It happens when we've lost sight of the simple sacred. This fire on our hearts that God is looking for is steady and continual not big and awesome. Steady and continual is how we carry wonder in our hearts.

Jesus will keep you steady in wonder. If you get a taste of raw glory, you'll be ruined for life. Sure, you'll have moments where grace is abounding to draw away with God more than other times. You'll have seasons where you are busier than others. Life happens to us all. But a wonder-filled person doesn't just want life happening to them. The wonder that Jesus awakens in our hearts encourages us to rise and *happen* to life.

I hope you'll recover your sense of wonder. I hope you'll remember that walking with Jesus is an adventure, a journey into uncharted waters. I hope you'll adventure beyond the edges of your devotional map. I hope you'll resolve to pursue the King and His promises until they are in your hands. I hope this book has nudged you to steal away with Jesus as it has for me as I wrote it. I think I'll steal away to Patmos and make lightning. I wonder if He'll give me a glimpse, a whisper, a fragrance to draw me in? I wonder what will happen there? I wonder.

## End Notes _____

[1] Donald T. Phillips, Martin Luther King, Jr. On Leadership (Warner Books: New York, 1999) p. 121.

[2] Craig Brian Larson, 750 Engaging Illustrations for Preachers, Teachers, and Writers, (Baker Books: Grand Rapids, 2007) p. 93.

## Bibliography _____

Larson, Craig Brian. *750 Engaging Illustrations for Preachers, Teachers, and Writers.* Grand Rapids: Baker Books Grand Rapids, 2007.

Phillips, Donald T. *Martin Luther King, Jr. On Leadership.* New York: Warner Books, 1999.

Made in the USA
Lexington, KY
02 August 2019